The Esoteric Meaning in Raphael's Paintings

THE PHILOSOPHY OF COMPOSITION IN

❖ The Disputa ❖ The School of Athens

❖ The Transfiguration

GIORGIO I. SPADARO

LINDISFARNE BOOKS
2006

Published by Lindisfarne Books
610 Main Street
Great Barrington, MA 01230
www.lindisfarne.org

ISBN: 1-58420-037-5

Library of Congress Cataloging-in-Publication Data is available.

10 9 8 7 6 5 4 3 2 1

Printed in the United States of America

Contents

Preface

MY INTENT in discussing three of Raphael's major paintings – the *Disputa (La Disputa)*, the *School of Athens (La Scuola di Atene)*, and the *Transfiguration (La Trasfigurazione)* – is to illuminate the esoteric meaning of the elements of composition used by Raphael, and not, as many have already done, to set the paintings in their historical contexts. Detailed information about the size, date, commission, execution and completion of each work is readily available in reference books for anyone interested in those aspects of Raphael's work and life. The bibliography at the end of this work lists several sources that provide descriptive commentary and traditional interpretations.

I am interested, however, in presenting the geometrical forms which underlie the compositional elements of Raphael's work and their importance in understanding the artist's message. An elaboration on the geometry used by Raphael, such as the Neoplatonic Academy in Florence, is beyond the scope of this writing. The compositions used in the three paintings discussed here go beyond the paintings themselves because they contain unique elements of not only esoteric Christian philosophy, but of religions or beliefs that have governed the social as well as the individual life of every human being. This is what I will endeavor to clarify. Many critics credit the environment in which Raphael was raised, Urbino and Florence during the Renaissance, for the way awareness of the spiritual realm influenced his artistic depiction of humankind's efforts toward enlightenment. However, other critics have stated that the spiritual world worked through Raphael's soul to bring to a visual consciousness the efforts of humankind toward enlightenment. These three paintings bring to our consciousness the wisdom that operated through Raphael. When examined as a group, they also provide the beholder with insight into the progression of his compositional efforts.

In discussing each painting I will purposely ignore some of the figures and other pictorial elements and details, which at this time are only corollary to my overall purpose. However, at the end of the analysis of each painting there is a list of names traditionally used to identify figures.

In the discussion that follows I will name only some of the painted figures who represent leaders of humanity. These figures are individuals whose thinking has shaped our lives. It is worthwhile to see where and how Raphael placed those particular figures. The placement and the countenance of the figures indicate what Raphael thought about them.

In the *Transfiguration,* for example, I am less concerned with identifying the standing woman in the foreground who looks at the epileptic child than with examining how her figure functions to direct one's attention toward the child. My humble purpose is to initiate a dialogue concerning the hidden qualities of Raphael's art and to leave further interpretation to future writers.

It has been pointed out to me that Raphael did not consciously create the compositions that I will elucidate. I agree with this, and this confirms that an artist's conscious effort is only one part of his or her task. During their creative activity, suddenly they know that they have become an instrument through which the spiritual world reveals itself.

My interest in Raphael was engendered in 1941 and 1945 when I visited the Vatican Museums with my cousin Beppe Assenza, a painter. What we discussed has not only resounded in my life, but has become a self-evident truth, expanding in meaning and complexity. Now I have the compelling need to share this knowledge.

Giorgio I. Spadaro

Introduction

Composition is our natural need to arrange and re-arrange specific components of the physical world around us. This act of composing is part of our everyday experience but often goes unnoticed or is seen as trivial activity. For example, we move the furniture in our rooms or house from one place to another. We compose our bodies for a certain activity, adopting a different physical attitude for a family meal as opposed to a formal dinner. Similarly, when performing, a dancer transforms a daily activity such as walking into an artistic communication appropriate for a particular performance. A dancer endeavors to communicate a sense of perfectly balanced grace calculated to hold our attention and make us marvel. We each require, and should seek, a period of time to recompose ourselves when a particular event has disarranged our normal balance.

Artists who have trained and heightened their innate sensitivity use composition to bring scattered elements into a coherent, meaningful communication to produce an aesthetic effect. When we first look at a painting, we are immediately aware of its colors and forms. Yet effort is required to discover the underlying compositional structure by which artists determine the use of certain colors, forms and lines. Raphael's paintings are no exception. Initially we are awed by their great size and quality, as well as by the artist's creative facility. Upon attentive inspection, the paintings' qualities become subordinate to the overall composition. The characteristics of the work – size, form, and color, among others – are disparate elements of the painting until they are visually engaged by the beholder. Through the interaction between the beholder and the work, the disparate elements merge into composition. During this interactive process, every element or quality that makes up the work becomes essential to the creation of composition from which the meaning of the work is derived.

In the *Disputa,* the painting is clearly divided into two main sections: the one above and the one below. Both of these sections are then divided into thirds: left, center, and right. In the lower part, Raphael skillfully uses linear perspective, an element of graphic communication, which came into consciousness in the fifteenth and sixteenth centuries. Raphael also felt the necessity of the leading thinkers of this period to bring to consciousness the physical aspect of the universe, and the earth in particular. The fact that Raphael was an admirer of many prominent artists, including Andrea Del Verrocchio and Leonardo, masters themselves of perspective, facilitated his skillful use of this visual device. In the upper section Raphael employs the traditional painting technique in which all the figures are painted as if existing on the same plane.

In the *School of Athens* we will see that perspective is further developed into a man-made structure, while in the *Transfiguration,* figures, landscape, and two separate events are manipulated to suit the artist's spatial composition to communicate his philosophical principles.

The uniqueness of Raphael's use of both the newer concept of perspective and the old format of juxtaposition of pictorial elements reveals the wisdom with which Raphael worked. He used these elements of composition to create balance and harmony in each painting, as well as to make a philosophical statement.

The composition of these paintings graphically communicates not only how the advent of Christianity relates to Western consciousness, but that it is a metamorphosed religious impulse originating in the East. For example, the perspective lines of the *Disputa* focus on the Host on the altar. By focusing on the physical element of a ritual, the spiritual realm is apprehended; we then realize the impact of the spiritual realm on the physical world. In the *School of Athens,* the spiritual activity of thinking is shown to shape the development of humankind and the human intellect across time. This time line – abscissa – travels from left to right. On this line a carrier of manuscripts travels and he exits on the right. This messenger carries past knowledge into the present, and after being metamorphosed by the present, new knowledge is brought into the future. Below this time line base, two streams of knowledge emerge: Christianity on the left beneath Apollo representing Love, and Science on the right, below Athena, representing wisdom. The spiritual and natural realms intersect again in the *Transfiguration,* where complex compositional elements must be considered before any interpretation is attempted.

Unfortunately, Raphael has been neglected or misunderstood by art critics. This last painting gave them the opportunity to criticize him for his miscarried composition, his ignorance, and many other negative attributes, which have made the inexperienced viewer shy away from pursuing an understanding of the intrinsic quality of his paintings.

❖ The Disputa ❖ The School of Athens

❖ The Transfiguration

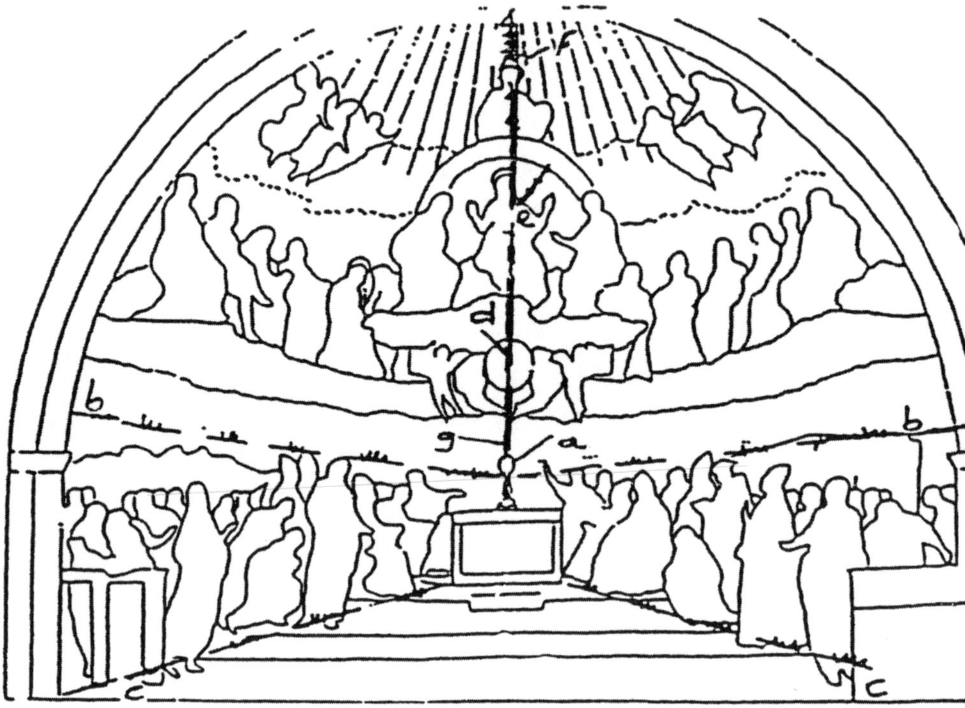

Figure 1

The Disputa

Many people will view Raphael's work through reproductions in art books, though some will see slides in an art class, and a few will actually stand before the originals. The latter viewers will have the advantage of seeing the *Disputa* as it was meant to be seen – from a point of view below the bottom line of the painting itself. It is from this point of view that the following discussion takes place.

Standing below the center of the *Disputa* in the Stanza della Segnatura, a former courtroom, the viewer will realize that the very bottom of the painting is above the average eye-level height. Therefore, by raising the eyes, the viewer first becomes aware of the horizontal lines depicting steps leading to the altar and thus to the round Sacred Host. Even though this circle depicting the Host is very small in comparison to the great size of the painting, it is of major importance because it serves as the focal point of perspective in the lower part of this painting (Figure I-a).

The Host, the perspective focal point, is the conclusion of two virtual lines which begin at the far left and far right edges of the painting and conclude at the Sacred Host. From the left side, along the top edge of the landscape and the figures' heads, runs a line to the Sacred Host.

Similarly, from the right, starting at the far side of the building, the line follows the figures' heads directly to the Host. There are also bottom lines from the left and right which follow the feet of the figures, but instead of intersecting at the Sacred Host, they merge at the base of the altar. The earthly environment of the painting's foreground is laid with the perspective lines mentioned above and the horizontal lines of the steps leading to the altar. The duality of left and right, of these two groups of figures is encompassed by the upper part of this painting. Even though the figures in this upper part are painted on a left-to-center and right-to-center fashion, the composition is based on an all-embracing curve. Therefore, while the lower part of the painting is based on perspective, the upper part is based on segments of circles, lemniscates, and ellipses, an echo of the cosmos.

Raphael's use of circles and segments thereof has a unique philosophical meaning as relates to the overall composition of the painting. The circle represents an earthly representation of time: no beginning or end. The segment of a circle as depicted here is but a portion of this universal time, and therefore the scene presented is valid for only this particular segment of earthly time in this particular locale.

Above the earthly environment, we have a scene of spiritual activities, in which the composition is laid on segments of curves. These curves bring into the painting a cosmic activity, as only in our minds can we complete the missing parts of a circle, lemniscate or hyperbola. Through this activity the soul of the viewer becomes active in a very specific way, complementing the physical vision with inner vision and creating meaning through composition. The composition here is intended to generate soul activity rather than just an intellectual perception.

As the various curved lines on which the viewer can see spiritual events progress down toward the altar, representing the earth, they flatten into horizontal lines and come to rest at the steps' lines below the altar. Within the framework established by the implicit lines of this earthly environment are individuals who have led the spiritual development of humankind. (FigureI-b–c). The identity of each of these figures, while interesting and worthy of further discussion, is not pertinent to an understanding of Raphael's compositional goals in the *Disputa* (See Figure 4 and the list of names with descriptions on pp. 38–43).

Once the viewer is focused on the Sacred Host, one cannot help but become aware that the Host is part of a series of increasingly larger circular motifs. The next circle above the host contains a dove, the Holy Spirit; the dove is painted on an appropriately golden background, for gold is the physical splendor of spiritual light (FigureI-d). Above this only half of the next larger circle is visible. This circle surrounds the figure of Christ and almost encompasses Mary, the

Mother of Jesus and John the Baptist (Figure I-e). Outside this circle and just above it is the Father figure with a quadrangular hat of which only two sides and three corners are visible (Figure I-f). Esoteric geometry tells us that the circle is the symbol of the spiritual activity of the cosmos, while the square is the symbol of the physical activity of the cosmos. The Father represents thinking, the continuous activity of human minds, which allows both physicality and spirituality to come into our consciousness.

Recognizing the Host as the starting point for this series of circles leading the viewer's eye to the Father figure, it becomes obvious that the Host, besides being the perspective focal point of the painting's lower half, is also the focal point of the spiritual hierarchies organized along a vertical line. The line runs upward from the Host through the other circles to the apex of the Father's pointed hat. This ascending vertical (Figure I-g) corresponds to a spiritual awareness prompted by the Host, visible only through the efforts of the individual who develops the ability to perceive the transparency of the material world. The Sacred Host, the earthly symbol of the Holy Spirit, simultaneously calls attention to itself and directs one's gaze upward to the spiritual hierarchies whose impulses govern humankind. If we consider the steps leading to the altar as a symbol of an upward metaphysical step involving knowledge and discipline, we can deduce that a progressive knowledge through the acquisition of the Host is a necessary step toward awareness.

The blessing Father figure above the half circle is painted on a gold background containing lines (rays) coming down from a source, which can only be imagined as existing outside the painting. Traditionally, the gold background– applied as uniformly as possible by the old masters, including the creators of Byzantine mosaics – served as a device to symbolize the splendor of light, the splendor of God. This splendor screened the spiritual world from being directly perceived. Only individuals who transcended the physical through esoteric disciplines could penetrate the spiritual mysteries to identify the various spiritual hierarchies that govern humans, animals, plants, and minerals. Here, however, Raphael modulates this gold background with lines, and between the lines he depicts spiritual beings. The streams of golden light rays filled with spiritual activity indicate that the spiritual world is no longer inaccessible to the human mind (Figure 2-a).

Having reached the top of the painting, the eyes of the beholder are directed downward by the rays. The beholder needs to imagine that the section of gold surface seen here is the lower portion of an infinitely large ellipse whose centers are outside the painting. Noticeable then, in the middle of this infinite gold section, is the Father figure, with his quadrangular hat, flowing white hair, violet and blue garments, and his right hand blessing the earth, which is held with his left. The shape of his garments also echoes the triangular form created by the hat. When the two sides of the hat are extended downward

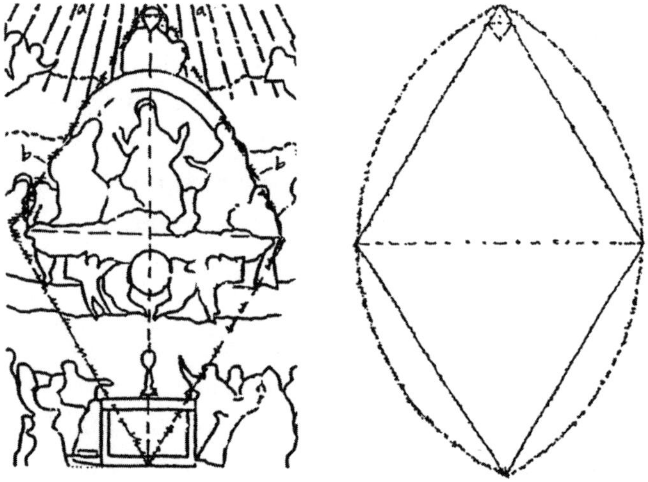

FIGURE 2

(Figure 2-b) they will meet a horizontal line on which the feet of Mary, Jesus, and John are resting. Inverting this virtual triangle we find that its apex touches the altar base. In the bisecting line of these virtual triangles, starting from the head of the Father and passing through the Sacred Host held in the ostensorium on the altar to the altar's base, we see the vertical disposition of the trinity – the Father, Son and Holy Spirit. The bisection of these triangles also reveals a feminine left side represented by Mary, and a masculine right side as represented by John the Baptist.

By re-examining the quadrangular hat we find that by drawing a line from the left side corner to the right, we have one triangle and its reflection. This quadrangular form with the hypotenuse cutting across the face of the Father can be considered the seed for the greater quadrangular form extending from hat to altar base and embracing the mother, Jesus, John the Baptist and five spiritual beings (Figure 2). The rhomboid shape of this great square can be considered the vesica-pisces, or spiritual envelope – an envelope, a sheath of spiritual light, containing the one spiritual activity which divides and multiplies itself. All this philosophical geometry can serve as a base for a meditation through which one can experience the great spiritual opposites: material and immaterial worlds, consciousness and unconsciousness, female and male, yin and yang.

At the bottom of the gold background is the first segment of a circle (Figure 3-a – b). This curve is a technical pictorial necessity which holds viewers in the painting and moves their attention down toward the bottom of it. If this curve, along with the ellipse described by the lower clouds, were not there, and if viewers focused their attention on the Sacred Host and then on the Holy Spirit, Christ and the Father, the Father's hat would visually carry the viewers out of the painting, distracting them from its intention. The golden line rays streaming from heaven and the curves redirect their attention back into the painting. The Father Figure, placed at the apex of the rhomboid, represents the human ability to think. Here the Father is placed in front

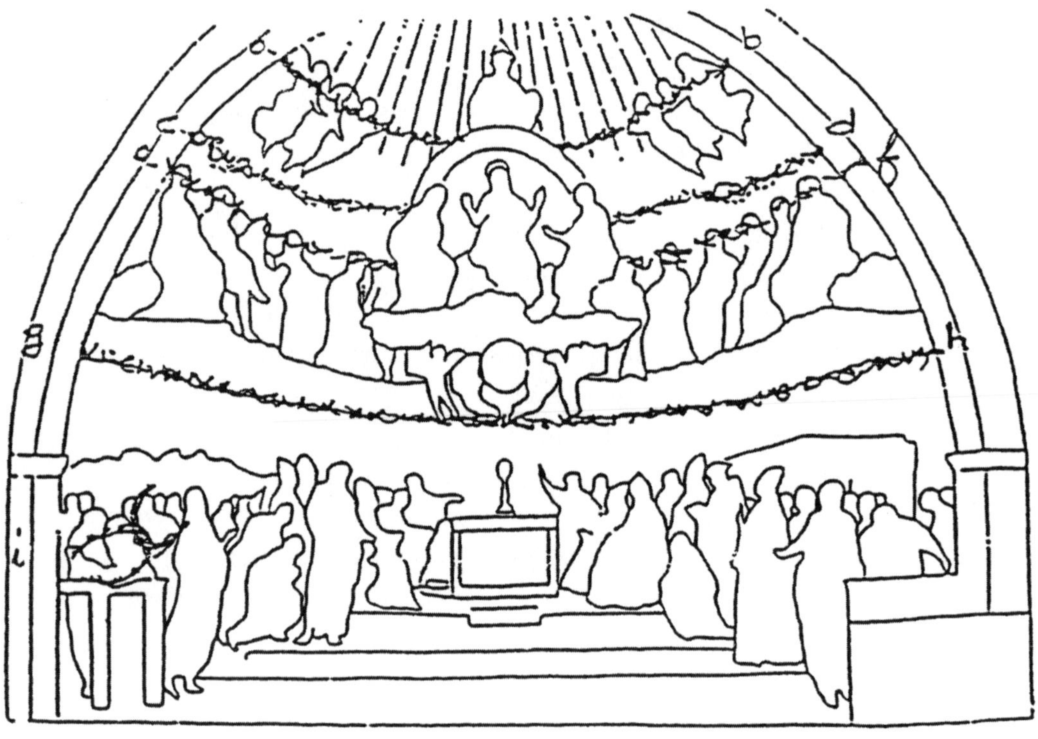

FIGURE 3

of a golden spiritual screen that could seem distant and inaccessible. However, Raphael mediates this space between heaven and thinking with lines of golden rays. Therefore, it is possible for the thinking mind to intuitively apprehend the mysteries of heaven.

On each side of the Holy Father are three winged figures whose gesturing arms and upper bodies are painted mostly over the gold background, with their lower bodies painted over clouds filled with spiritual beings. Traditionally, angelic creatures were represented as belonging to only one realm – the heavenly. Raphael has instead chosen to depict these spiritual beings as simultaneously part of two aspects of the spiritual worlds. Rudolf Steiner, in reference to esoteric teachings, suggests that the Logos (or Word) was made up of seven Elohim (Rishis), the hierarchy above the Angels, Archangels, and Archai. The six figures on the border of the golden area are the six Elohim remaining in the spiritual world after the Christ's incarnation; Christ himself is the seventh one.

The spiritual beings in the ribbon of clouds underneath the gold area are *putti;* innocent, passionless souls who guard the threshold leading to the higher spiritual activity. They are part of another ellipse whose curve is flatter than the ellipse of gold (Figure 3-c – d). Flatter still is the curve formed by the more terrestrial blue sky and clouds against which the heads of leaders – patriarchs – of humankind are painted (Figure 3-e – f). Finally, the lowest ribbon of clouds, filled with darker painted *putti,* indicates the first threshold of initiation, dividing the earthly from the spiritual world. The top of this ribbon is related more to the higher composition as evidenced by the smaller diameter of the curve. The bottom line of these clouds is related more to the earthly environment; the curve is of a larger diameter, flattening on each end (Figure 3-g – h).

Beautifully integrated into this bottom layer of clouds are four *putti*, two on either side of the Holy Spirit circle. Each one holds one of the four gospels. The *putti* on the far right and left each have one foot on a small cloud that functions as a symbolic ground, indicating the transition from a physical environment to a spiritual way of knowing. This group of four figures is close to the earth, their open books above the altar offering humankind a way to spiritual knowledge. These *putti* and their books, placed under his feet, are subordinate to Christ but create a bridge from which he may be reached. These Gospels that flank the dove, which is placed on a gold background, are heralding the possibility of experiencing the Christ through reading the scripture. The dove, placed in gold background, also represents the possibility of attaining Christ through reading. The golden background behind the dove symbolizes the splendor of light, whereas the dove in white represents the image of light, just as the four nearby Gospels represent the image of the writer's thinking. The other way to reach Christ, also presented on the right side of the painting, is through direct perception, which is a gift given to a few individuals such as artists and philosophers.

Between the lowest threshold of clouds and the lines of human figures on the earth is a blue sky. In the landscape, on the left side, humans are involved in the activity of village life, unconcerned with the spiritual debate of the foreground. On the right side is a building, an enclosure that traditionally symbolizes the human skull. A polarity is thus established between the rural, natural flow and the accomplished, purposeful activity of the human mind shown through limb activity and head activity, as well as through the building. The contents of this building are depicted in the *School of Athens.*

The altar links the right and left halves of the lower portion. The polarity between these two halves reflects the structure of the human mind. The feminine left side portrays devotion: the woman in prayer, the books to be read lying closed, and human activity taking place within nature. The schools of thought and groups of people are framed within the natural environment, showing a passive relationship to the divine. By contrast, books are written on the masculine right side. The woman in pink, the color of incarnation, is bringing to consciousness what is born in the mind of Augustine (the figure to her right who is asking her to write). On the right, the emphasis is on the emergence from the physical building which predominates over the symbolic landscape. The individuals are isolated from the landscape.

Raphael ties together the two activities, the left and the right, with horizontal lines in the form of steps progressing toward the altar, representing the progression toward the spiritual realm. Horizontal parallel lines symbolize time, the stages of consciousness mounting upward. Therefore, different aspects of human pursuit stand within measurable time. In contrast to this is an all-embracing spiritual activity composed of curves, symbols of universal, immeasurable time.

The polarity between the left and right sides of the painting, is an obvious division between the upper and lower spheres of activity – the spiritual and earthly. It is important to see that the compositional structures represent the differences between the two spheres: the earthly is angular and linear (dividing), while the spiritual is curved (encompassing).

Our minds can easily comprehend that the curve of a lemniscate symbolically describes infinity, and that an ellipse transforms itself into straight lines when on earth. A line between two points on the Earth is actually a curve because of the spherical shape of the Earth. However, between two close points the line appears straight from an earthly perspective and curved from a heavenly perspective. The ellipse, or a segment thereof – a curve – and the straight line are elements emphasized in this painting. And just as we are aware of the symbolic meaning of elliptical segments, we are also aware of the meaning of lines. What we call a straight line is limited to earthly concepts and serves as an expression of the material world. Straight lines are created by humans as a system of logic through which we may describe our surrounding world. Within the space enclosed by lines and the first curve formed by the clouds are painted individuals who, through their contributions to the arts and humanities, are leaders of humanity.

In contrast, the curves invite us to imagine how they encompass the universe, yet the confines of the painting remind us that we are looking at only one segment of a totality. These segments carry the imagination into cosmic activity and Raphael seems to indicate that Christianity is only one aspect of a cosmic activity, implying that there are other existing spiritual activities that do not presently concern us at this stage of human development, although they exist nonetheless. Christianity is a spiritual activity designed for one particular aspect of human development.

Now we have traced the series of progressively flatter ellipse segments from the top curve where the gold ends, down the stages of spiritual activity, to its final resting place on the two top perspective lines of the painting's lower section. These lines, proceeding from the left and right, converge centrally at the Host in its Ostensorium on the altar, as can be seen in Figure I-b.

Raphael's use of perspective denotes a sequential development of a particular activity. The spiritual world is seen as a spatial activity where the elements of the composition are juxtaposed to each other and can be seen simultaneously with the use of the viewer's imagination. Like his sixteenth-century contemporaries, Raphael introduced the material world into art with the use of perspective. Raphael brings together the old methods of juxtaposing figures in the space of a painting and the new method of drawing figures in perspective.

The first one is a spiritual activity presented in a graphic mode; the second one is a spiritual activity filtered through earthly environments. By using both modes on the same surface he indicates that the material world is a reflection of the spiritual world. He informs us that it is possible to imagine that the physical world is one aspect of the spiritual. This is further demonstrated through the linking of the two worlds through the vertical hierarchy from the Host to the Father figure.

Once the compositional elements of the painting, from bottom to top and back again, and from left to right, have been absorbed, viewers will naturally shift their gaze from left to right along the lower horizontal plane. At this point I want to remind the reader that the narration of the figures hereafter described can be challenged. Calling one figure Bramante or Raphael is less important than acknowledging what the gestures, the color of their garments, and the countenance mean to the painting in terms of their contribution to the overall composition.

As mentioned earlier, the group of individuals on the left-hand side is foregrounded against a landscape with buildings in various stages of completion. The builders are unconcerned with what is happening in the foreground. The colorful figures painted in the foreground and their gestures are below the perspective top line which goes from the far left to the Host (Figure I-b). These figures contained within the left side are receiving spiritual knowledge through cult, ritual, group activity, and the knowledge preserved in books. At the far left of the foreground are two figures who are disputing this knowledge, and these two figures give the painting its popular title, the *Disputa*. One is holding and pointing at a book while his gaze is directed to the altar. The other looks at the book over the first's shoulders while his hand points to the altar. A third figure in this group is a young man wearing an apprentice's cap; he is a student of the first two. These figures are connected not only by their apparent argument over the text, but by their gestures, designed to indicate a dynamic Cassini lemniscate – a figure eight (Figure 3-i), which is a recurrent compositional theme in Raphael's work that will be especially evident in the *Transfiguration*.

Traditionally, the figure holding the book, on whose right is the young figure wearing a pupil's hat, has been identified as Bramante, an architect and contemporary of Raphael. The figure looking over Bramante's shoulders is a graduate pupil disputing what Bramante is indicating. The presence of the apprentice in this dynamic group indicates that the argument is transferred into the future. The argument is also transferred forward through the golden seraphic figure standing nearby, as indicated through its body composition.

Not one gesture or activity of these figures crosses above the perspective line (Figure I-b) separating the lower section from the upper section. Consistent with the compositional structure, the gestures of the characters are always lower than, and thus subordinate to, the Sacred Host, to the Ritual-Ceremony (Faith). This indicates that one experiences the spiritual through the knowledge of books and through the Sacrament, the physical representations of the spiritual world. We may then deduce that the figures on the left side of the painting are individuals who, in combining their efforts with others, are destined to perceive the spiritual world through the ritual presented here as the Monstrance of the Sacred Host.

The characters on the left side of the painting's lower half are divided into three groups whose garments and attitudes show progress in esoteric development through the Church's sacred Ritual-Ceremony. The first group in the foreground of the left wears simple garments, symbolically indicating a basic soul activity. The next group has acquired a higher knowledge than the previous one, displayed by figures wearing miters. The group closest to the altar is profoundly absorbed in reading or in contemplation of the Sacred Host. Even though the gestures of this final group do not go beyond the top line of the perspective, the figures are closer to the Host, showing that this group has acquired even higher spiritual knowledge than the previous one.

On the lower half of the right side are artists, thinkers and theologians who stand on their own, in contrast to the three distinct groups on the left. These figures appear to have emerged from a building, an architectonic symbol of the human skull. Their emergence from this building indicates that in order to pursue spiritual knowledge, it is necessary for them to move away from the finite intellectual thinking inherent to materialism and into a more natural environment where intuition may be nurtured. Through heightened intuitive capabilities, these individuals see directly into the spiritual world. This is emphasized by the figure closest to the altar who reaches above the host with his right hand. His gesture prevents the perspective line from reaching the host and indicates via a pointed finger that the individuals on his left have direct communion with the spiritual world.

This individual has been identified as Leonardo da Vinci, whose firm gesture points directly to the spiritual world and transcends the Monstrance, implying that a direct connection to the spiritual world is possible without the need for ritual. This is confirmed by the fact that Raphael painted most of these figures against an architectural structure that symbolizes the human mind and by his choice of figures. Whether through art, science, or philosophy, each of these figures has contributed to the ability of humans to connect with the spiritual world as individuals. By clustering these individuals on the right side, in the embrace of Leonardo's gesture, Raphael elevates the artist and thinker to the highest level of human spiritual endeavor. This side represents the notion that thinking precedes feeling, and that through intellect one may access the spiritual. The figures on the right stand individually, in contrast to those on the left who search for knowledge through the words and ideas of others.

The figures on the left side of the painting are focused on the Sacred Host, showing that they must go through a Ritual-Ceremony to perceive the spiritual world. In the Ritual-Ceremony, feeling is predominant; this refers to an educated sense of feeling and therefore is removed from instinct and arbitrariness. The attention of the collection of figures on the right, however, is directed toward the gesture of the man closest to the altar who points directly to the spiritual world. This would mean that those individuals with refined artistic, intuitive abilities are capable of directly perceiving the spiritual activity according to their individual efforts and not as a group effort, in contrast with those on the left. Implicit in these contrasts is the notion that in order to have an individual, direct relationship to Christianity, it is necessary to move away from other people's knowledge and to trust in one's own educated, nurtured intuition.

Between the left and the right side of the lower half of the painting stands the altar, whose stones frame a surface decorated with a mandala of the endless knot. The mandala stands for the pursuit of self-knowledge through which we perceive the world; placed as it is here, it is the center of self-knowledge. The mandala is the simplest ancient symbol, which would enable or generate a thinking activity necessary to visualize the balancing of the two opposites, the conscious or physical and the unconscious or spiritual. Placed here, the mandala represents the visible development of logic as understood by those of the Eastern tradition.

The mandala is also contained into the myth of the Minotaur. In the Greek myth, Ariadne's thread allows Theseus to conquer the monster at the labyrinth's center. The labyrinth stands as a symbol of the human brain's circumvolutions. Theseus conquers the monster and sails home, mistakenly allowing the new impulse of knowledge to live. Through this myth's interpretation of the mandala, we see that our thinking is brought to quality by the thread of logic.

The altar represents Western influence as opposed to the Eastern element of the mandala. It is through the grouping of these two symbols that we are able to see the development of Christianity and logic in the Western consciousness: the Eastern foundation represented by the mandala being transformed into a Western way of understanding represented by the altar.

The mandala is the symbol of a mental process of logic, which is, by all standards of knowing, imperceptible; it is occult, hidden. This logic is a necessary thinking process to enable us to navigate purposefully within thinking. Similar imagery lies in the Perseus-Ariadne myth, or in the story of Penelope, wife of Odysseus and queen of Ithaca, who metamorphosizes the thread into a weaving. At night the day's weaving must be unraveled.

This contrast is further represented by the two figures that are on either side of the altar. On the left, St. Francis, in the utmost visual communication of feeling, is prostrated next to the altar as if holding it up. This indicates a relationship based on feeling and a relationship with nature. On the right side as a counterpoint to St. Francis is Leonardo da Vinci, arm outstretched toward the heavens, emphasizing thought over feeling.

The mandala is a way to inwardly find the relationship between the visible and the hidden, or occult, which is the purpose of this painting. The *Disputa* itself combines the seen and unseen in perceptible form. The two activities of the human mind on either side of the altar are both valid ways of perceiving the spiritual. On the left, the ritual is experienced through a group, a church or a congregation; on the right is the individual's direct experience. Through them the spiritual world is communicated in the form of the arts and philosophy. Through both, a human being can know him or her self.

The altar as well as the Host is humankind's conscious effort to lift the earth toward the spiritual world, transforming the earthly material into something receptive to spiritual communication. The Monstrance on the altar holds the sacred Host, symbolizing Christ's sacrifice through which humans can obtain spiritual knowledge. The circle around the Host is echoed by the circle of the Holy Spirit and by the circle inscribing the Christ, only one half of which is visible. Therefore, the circle of the Host stands for the physical self, which is expanding to the spiritual self.

So, from the Sacred Host, to the Holy Spirit, to the Christ we have circles inviting us to know ourselves. By placing the Monstrance on ancient wisdom, the mandala, Raphael presents to us a new form with which to know ourselves.

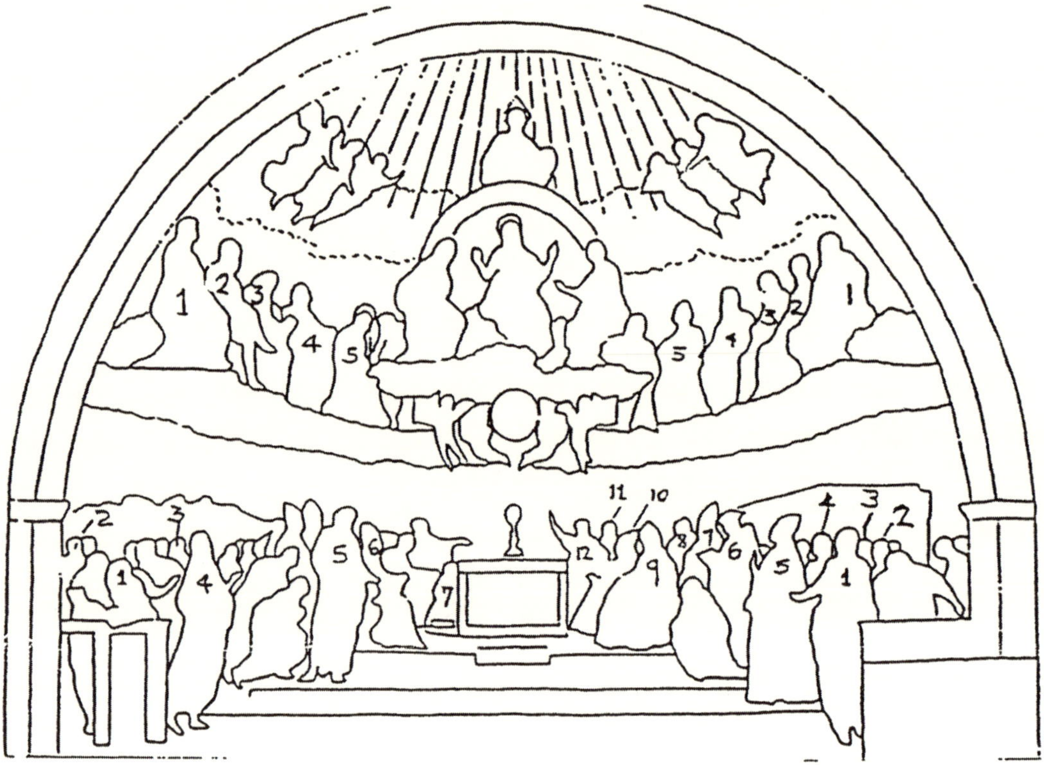

Figure 4

Identities Attributed by Critics to Figures in the *Disputa*

In the *Disputa,* Raphael presents characters in certain dress and colors, as well as with specific attitudes and expressions, which are relevant, albeit not the focus, and may assist the reader in obtaining a fuller understanding of the composition in the *Disputa.*

Lower Left

1. Bramante discussing the Sacred Scriptures with graduate pupil while another undergraduate looks on: Raphael emphasizes the intimacy and profound reciprocal communication between Bramante and the graduate by basing their bodily composition on a lemniscate.

2. Fra Angelico stares directly at the altar.

3. Julius II – Baldhead with well-groomed beard.

4. Graphic representation of a soul in pursuit of knowledge. Blue is the painter's traditional color to represent the soul. The outer blue garment represents the soul while the red and yellow garments show the soul's active pursuit of knowledge. The hand gesture at heart level indicates that the communication with the Host is accessed through feeling. The seraphic oval face, surrounded by golden locks of hair, turned to the left, communicates that the individual is looking behind to ancient wisdom. This figure concludes the first group.

5. This towering figure with his back turned to the viewer has been named Seneca, who translated Greek tragedies for Pope Julius II.

6. Pope Gregory the Great (540-604 A.D.) is seated on a throne with lion heads decorating the armrests. To the left of this seated figure are bishops reading and gesturing toward the altar.

7. Francis kneeling, praying while leaning against the altar as if to help support it.

8. Jerome contemplating the *Vulgate*.

LOWER RIGHT

1. Michelangelo – A godlike, muscular figure showing a pupil the way to the spiritual world.

2. Cosimo de Medici–Influential in Florentine life through financial support; the Medici activity brought to life the Platonic Academy, later known as the Biblioteca Medici Laurentiana, where it is said that the birth of the Renaissance took place.

3. Between Cosimo de Medici and Michelangelo, the hooded monk facing the viewer is Savonarola, who was the prior of San Marco Monastery in Florence.

4. Dante with laurels on his head and a godlike profile. Raphael de-emphasized the actual bridge of Dante's nose as seen in an earlier sketch to stress the god and goddess quality of human form before

the advent of intellectuality. Dante is placed next to Michelangelo to show the influence of Dante on Michelangelo.

5. To Dante's right, wrapped in gold garments and looking directly at the spiritual world, is Pope Sextus IV (1471-1484).

6. Bonaventura, wearing a cardinal red hat and Franciscan garb, was canonized in 1482 by Sextus.

7. Pope Anacletus is the third pope. He holds a palm branch indicating martyrdom.

8. Thomas Aquinas, with a bare, broad head, absorbed in himself and wearing the Dominican habit.

9. Augustine, seated, holding a book on his knee with his right hand and with his left pointing to a woman who is writing his dictation.

10. Domenicus = St. Dominic (1181-1221) who was the founder of the Dominican Order of preachers to which the Franciscans objected.

    Ambrosius = Ambrosio (340-397), next to Augustine, is looking up at the spiritual realm. A powerful Northern Italian political figure (Bishop of Milan, 374-397), he composed church music, and his world awareness and compassion were the very elements which made Augustine become a Christian.

11. Leonardo da Vinci, with a great, sweeping, dramatic gesture, pointing at the Holy Ghost and, further, at the enthroned Christ.

Leonardo wears a garment that is the same green used in painting the altar antependium, background of the mandalic form, as well as the color of Socrates' garment in the *School of Athens*.

Upper Left

1. Peter, his feet solidly grounded, with a proportionally small head, holding a key.
2. Adam, placed next to Peter in the role of teacher, is meant to represent the old, while Peter represents the new.
3. John the Evangelist, author of the most esoteric Gospel, which emphasizes the importance of the Word. He is writing on a tablet, with his eyes semi-closed as if in an attitude of looking at inner visions.
4. David, wearing a crown on his peasant head-cover. He is holding a lyre, which stands for the poetic form of David's communication.
5. Lawrence, the martyr, wearing a violet tunic, the color of the mystic, his white undergarment indicating purity of soul.

Upper Right

1. The Apostle Paul in a mystically violet robe with a book and sword.
2. Abraham holding a sacrificial knife with his right hand, representing his willingness to sacrifice his son for God. His left hand steadies his right, symbolically indicating God's intervention.

3. Thought to be Jacob, older brother of St. James, because of his unmistakable resemblance to the figure of Christ. He is absorbed in himself.
4. Moses with laws on tablets. Two rays of light extend from his head. The two horns stand for that quality that permeates human thinking when it embraces spiritual as well as material thoughts.
5. Stephen, proto-martyr, who saw the spiritual world while being tortured.

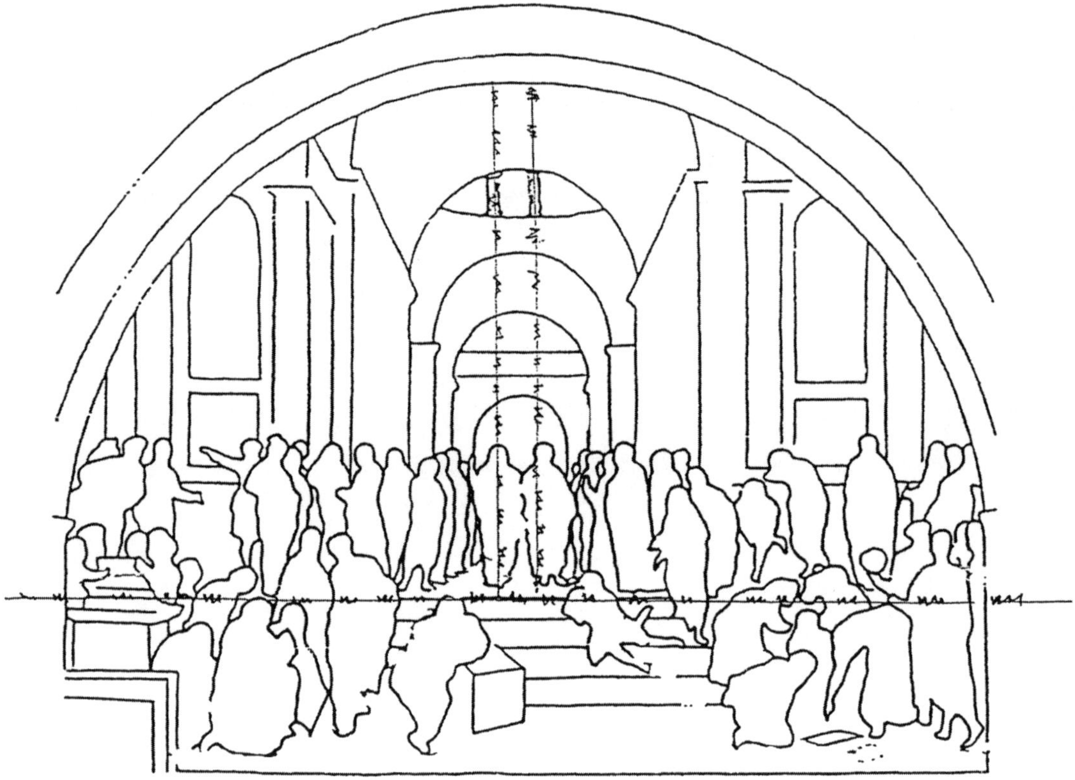

FIGURE 5

The School of Athens

On the wall opposite the *Disputa* we find the *School of Athens.* We could imagine that in the *School of Athens* Raphael illustrates what could go on inside the building located on the right side of the *Disputa.*

As is true for the *Disputa,* beholders of the *School of Athens* must raise their heads to view the painting. As the viewers' eyes are drawn upward to where the two central figures stand, they cannot ignore the two columns resting on the architrave of the second vault. These columns with the two figures below them form two imaginary vertical axis or coordinates. These two verticals rest on the line – abscissae – of the first of several steps which lead downward. Therefore it is easy to visualize that this upper part of the *School* is divided into left and right with a center space running between the two columns. The vaults with hexagonal coffering are divided by two columns, thus forming two hemispheres, a duality, an alternative, and therefore choice. These two columns symbolize a spiritual activity coming in – left column, and going out – right column. This dualism, which is inherent to knowledge, is the main theme of the *School of Athens* (Figure 5).

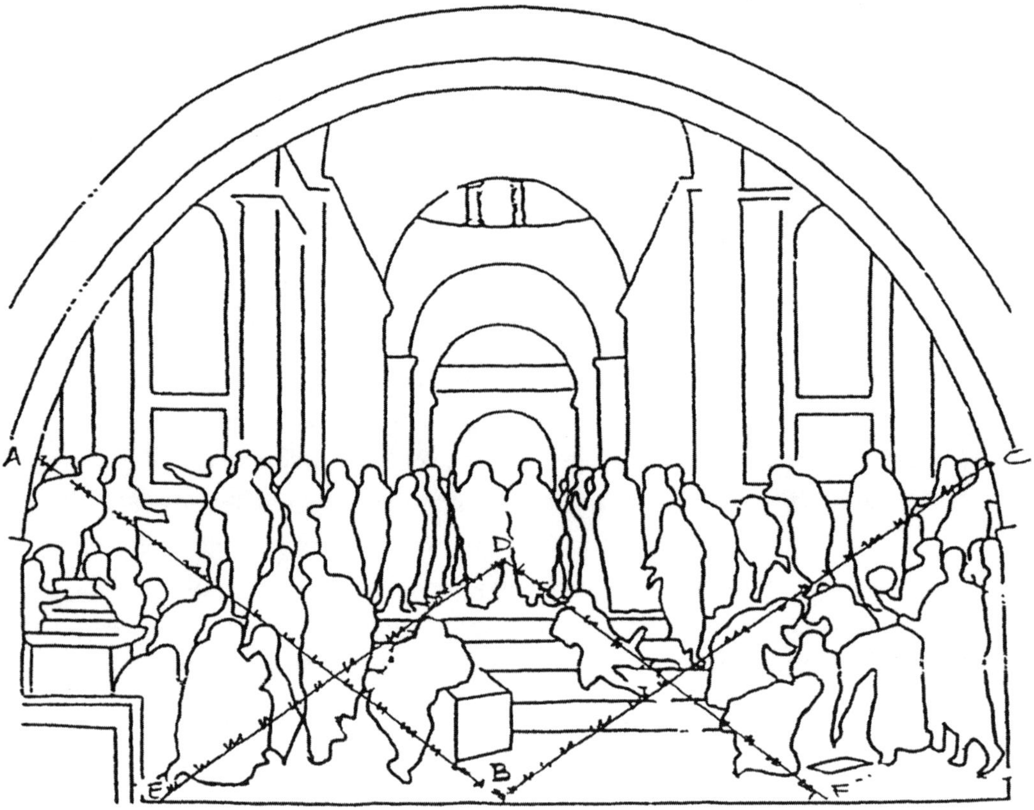

Figure 6

Above the base line – abscissae – are depicted people in various attitudes distributed along a horizontal ribbon, which runs across the entire painting.

Below this ribbon of human activity are figures painted within triangular spaces. These triangles are created by points A, B, and C combined with points D, E, and F. The overlapping of these two triangles creates a diamond shape at the base of the painting (Figure-6 ABCEDF).

The figures located within the confines of these spaces, while intent on their own activities, are not isolated from the larger ribbon of activity referred to previously.

To the left of Apex B a man is seated, on the right a man is sprawled on the steps. After this initial exploration of the geometric composition, our attention is redirected to the immediate foreground and to the seated figure. (See also Figure 7 and the list of identities attributed to figures in the *School of Athens*, pp. 68–70).

This seated man leaning on a block of marble is oblivious to his surroundings as he ponders his writing. The viewer is immediately aware of the great emphasis on the muscular legs and traveling boots. The soles of these boots and the shadows they cast are in the foreground closest to the viewer. A sense of motion is suggested by the figure, both because of his muscular physique, his intense concentration in writing, and his traveler's boots. His pose portrays thinking, which is the central theme of the painting, but emphasizes the outgoing aspect of thought, and in this case, communication through writing. He is not a man of graceful features. He is stocky and has broad shoulders and strong arms. He is a doer, a forger of activities and a traveler. He lives in the element of the will. From this we may deduce that this figure is the Apostle Paul. To emphasize Paul's importance, Raphael has placed him within this triangle and in the foreground as if he were ready to leap out of the painting and into action.

The other prominent figure in the middle area of the painting is sprawled on the steps, scantily clothed in a cerebral blue garment and reading a manuscript. This figure, identifiable as Diogenes, is oblivious to anything other than himself. Diogenes holds the manuscript as if it were a mirror. To the right of Diogenes is a figure climbing the steps, back turned to the beholder, hands pointing downward to the sprawling figure of Diogenes in an attempt to bring Diogenes to the attention of the figures above. Self-centered Diogenes stands for what could be knowledge for the sake of knowledge, the kind of intellectual reflective thinking that restricts or blinds the mind and limits creativity. Diogenes is resting on the steps, the lines of which can be interpreted as the graphic symbol of time, and of progression as in the *Disputa*. Diogenes is therefore blocking the flow of knowledge that is to be carried into the future. Raphael seems to warn that within schools of thought there is the possibility of self-centeredness, of oblivion to one's surroundings, reflecting only the knowledge from within the individual. When an individual is engrossed in a specific intellectual or scientific pursuit, it is possible to lose sight of the larger context of what is being studied, leading to self-aggrandizement. This aspect of academia is symbolized through the sheet of paper on which Diogenes concentrates, without ever seeming to notice that he is in the center of a busy location. Diogenes' body language is foretelling the coming of specialization, which will bring isolation and difficulties in communication between various branches of science.

Paul communicates his higher awareness to others through his writing and traveling. These two also reflect the tendencies of Plato and Aristotle. Paul is a sharp contrast to Diogenes. Both are contained within the steps of time or stages of cognition; however Diogenes is concerned only with his work and personal knowledge, without giving thought to passing knowledge into the future.

The central area occupied by Paul and Diogenes is, for the viewer, the entrance into the *School of Athens*. Paul exemplifies an attitude that invokes the importance of community-shared knowledge, seeking to develop the thinking that is required for progress and development, while Diogenes is the example that renders the community knowledge and future participation in thinking processes unimportant.

The *School of Athens* is a predominantly enclosed structure with three arches directing the viewer toward the sky at the far end of the building. These arches create three separate vaults, which represent a philosophical trinity comprised of thinking, feeling, and will. These arches are interspersed with swatches of blue sky, and their perspective lines descend toward the two main figures painted on a blue background with white clouds. The two columns at the top of the second vault, besides symbolizing a coming in and going out of spiritual activities, also create the duality that divides the school into a left and right side, similar to the left and right sides of the human brain. Plato, the figure on the left side, is gesturing with his index finger in the air, parallel to his head. This gesture indicates the words, "I am" or "one." The purple of Plato's undergarment symbolizes contemplation, while the shining red of his outer garment, with its downward lines and folds open toward Aristotle, signifies a contained will. The contemplative purple of Plato is echoed by the purple of Paul. Plato's feet are barely touching the ground as he walks, suggesting a kind of ethereal presence.

Aristotle, who is welcoming Plato into the School of Athens, is dressed in a blue garment. This color, in this context, suggests cerebral activity, and in contrast to Plato, Aristotle's feet are not only very visible, but are planted firmly on the ground pointing slightly toward the right.

Plato is carrying his book, the *Timaeus,* and Aristotle is carrying his *Ethics.* The writings of these two individuals have become the basis for two schools of thought that have fundamentally shaped most of Western thinking, Platonism and Aristotilialism. Although these two individuals dominate the *School* because of their centered location, they are part of a stream of individuals depicted on the same level on either side of them spanning the main floor. Distributed on the three steps below this fascia of figures are two large groups of figures on the left and right, representing these two schools of thought.

These two central figures are also painted inside the building openings through which the sky is visible. The clouds represent a threshold, similar to the clouds in the *Disputa*. but unlike in the *Disputa*, with its depiction of the heavenly sphere, here Raphael describes only human cognition below such a spiritual threshold. The left and right side walls of this building have niches with Greek figures painted in a monochrome color indicating that though they are threads of the past, they are still influential. On the left side is the figure of Apollo, thus the left side is referred to as the Apollonian side.

Apollo is god of poetry, harmony, and medicine, and Plato is considered a son of Apollo, healing the soul with his words. Therefore, the left half of the *School* represents the Apollonian line of Greek philosophy, dedicated to searching for harmony and proportion, finding goodness in beauty, bettering humankind with the force of ethics. On the pedestal holding Apollo's statue is a bar-relief depicting youthful figures dancing or frolicking. Below this, at the very base of the pedestal, is painted a sexual orgy. The primordial force of creation, sex, depicted here shows that there cannot be beauty without this maligned natural creativity which unites male and female in unison to experience the sacredness of life. The progression from the very base of this pedestal to the Apollo statue is a progression to joy and love.

In the right side niche, usually referred to as the Minervian side, is Athena. As the brainchild of Zeus, she presides over the pursuit of knowledge. Athena/Minerva, is the goddess of wisdom and science. Aristotle was the philosopher of science, searching for the nature of causes and the causes of nature. For Aristotle, education of youth played a special role. It comes as no surprise that education occupies a prominent role on the right side of the *School of Athens.*

On the pedestal holding Athena/Minerva is painted a domestic scene indicating that the goddess is the protector of family or community.

Although these two Greek god and goddess figures seem to decorate or simply blend into the background of the painting, they are guiding principles through which the viewer may better understand Raphael's intention. The figures may represent soul forces within the individual, so that the *School of Athens* is not only a picture of a historical setting, but also a picture of the ongoing pursuit toward knowledge.

Raphael positioned Plato and Aristotle looking in each other's direction, indicating that these two streams of thinking were coming together in the Renaissance. Plato is painted as though he is poised to move forward, as if the essence of his thinking cannot be understood from within a confined physical environment; and therefore it is necessary to move away from the kind of logical and intellectual thinking that limits the boundary of creativity so that inspiration, imagination, and intuition can be nurtured. This concept is echoed on the right-hand side of the *Disputa* where the individuals come out of the building into the open space to perceive the spiritual world.

Aristotle is looking at Plato, his right hand motioning out toward the school and parallel to the ground. This horizontal gesture is in direct counterpoint to Plato's vertical gesture. The two gestures together form a cross, combining the upward gesture of the spiritual world with the outward gesture of the physical. By having Aristotle hold his *Ethics,* Raphael emphasizes this Aristotelian quality of activity on the physical plane of existence. Aristotle's blue robe and gold-trimmed brown garment symbolize the aspect of thinking applied to perception of the outer world. Ideas and thoughts no longer exist only in the heavenly realm, but are also conditioned by our senses and the physical world. Aristotle's left foot is pointing outward, askew from the axis of his figure and away from Plato. This deviation from Platonic thinking that Aristotelian thinking brought to consciousness is a deviation necessary for the birth of natural science. Plato's own nature prevented him from understanding this type of thinking. Raphael, by depicting Aristotle this way, reveals the importance of Aristotelian philosophy to the Renaissance and the future.

The image of Plato and Aristotle coming in the school from the blue background of the sky may be seen as an archetypal thought form of western consciousness. This view of humanity makes us understand that we are to relate to the heavenly as well as the earthly realm.

Though Aristotle seems to be looking at Plato, it is also possible to interpret his gaze as looking past Plato at a young man with his arms crossed over his chest who is looking with devotion toward Aristotle. His countenance displays youthful and agile energy. The richness of his garments, including his golden sandals and his noble posture, mark him as Alexander the Great. The education Alexander received from Aristotle allowed him to envision a world where everyone was equal. Greek education spread throughout the empire of Alexander and became the essential foundation of Christianity.

Similarly, Plato's gaze passes across Aristotle to a group of figures, singling out a powerful-looking, old man, bald and bearded, who wears a heavy shining yellow garment that reaches to the floor. Instead of looking at Plato, this man looks across toward Alexander. Compared to this figure, Aristotle and Plato look young in character. The old man stands expectantly, waiting to receive what these young philosophers have to offer. He is Xenophon of Colophaus, also known as Xenophon from Ilea in southern Italy. He is the founder of the Ileatic school of philosophy, which taught that everything came from earth. This is one reason why Raphael painted his garment in one color, yellow, the color of knowledge, with just a small portion of green, the color of the Earth. Nevertheless, Xenophon disregarded all the anthropomorphic Greek gods by stating that there was only one god who was not human and did not think like humans. Xenophon's philosophy, while not anticipating the incarnation of the Son of God – Jesus Christ – influenced Western thinking until the Middle Ages. To his right, the figure with a raised hand is Parmenides, a student of Xenophon who stands there as if to confirm Xenophon's philosophy.

Between the group usually identified with Socrates to the left of Plato and Aristotle are several lesser figures whose attention is focused on the two great thinkers.

On the Apollonian side a messenger rushes in carrying a scroll (antiquity) and a book (modernity). This messenger is invited into the School by a guardian, wearing a hat, and is welcomed by the next figure. Old and new knowledge is welcomed in the school. The messenger delivers knowledge to the individuals painted on the time line – abscissae – and these individuals contribute their own impulses and transform this knowledge, and this knowledge is carried into the future by the exiting figure on the far right. That the entering messenger is depicted with his head turned away from the viewer, while the exiting messenger looks back into the school, seems to demonstrate a progression from anonymous to individualized knowledge. Upon entering the epoch of thinking shown in the *School of Athens*, the messenger is clothed in orange, which may signify courage. At the time of leaving, the messenger no longer carries writings, but has become clothed with knowledge, evidenced by his garment of purple and red. With gesture, body, and color, Raphael portrays the development of learning in the school through time, or the evolution of human thought. The balance created through the distribution of figures and the overall composition of the painting creates a harmony through which one may begin to make sense of the metamorphosis of knowledge. In an attempt to better understand the metamorphosis of knowledge in the creation of balance, it will be necessary to study the figures depicted in the *School of Athens* and their relationships to one another.

The group to the lower left forms a triangle with the line starting at the messenger coming in and ending where Paul is seated resting his left elbow on a marble block. This group of figures conveys important knowledge concerning Christianity. To the left of Paul another figure intently writes, but he writes as if he needs more to remember than to think. This writer is Mark; however he has been mistakenly identified by J. D. Passavant as Pythagoras, an error, which has colored the interpretation of this group.

Luke's identity comes from the fact that he is wearing elegant clothing – a fine green garment and a turban – which distinguish him as a professional. In contrast, below Luke are Matthew and Mark in their humble garb. Luke and Matthew are attentively looking at

Mark's writing, and we know that these three are the authors of the synoptic Gospels. While reading what Mark is writing, Luke displays his emotion by holding his right hand over his heart.

In the top left corner we have a messenger who carries scrolls and a book, symbols of past and future knowledge, respectively. It is fair to speculate that by depicting the life of Christ below the messenger, Raphael indicates that Christianity's influence is an important part of future knowledge that must be passed on. Through the bodily composition of the messenger we see that he appears to be in a rush, running with a sense of anxiety about his mission.

Below the messenger and to his right, is a laurel-crowned head indicating that this person is an artist. In old Greece the artist was a person with natural qualities, which distinguished him from others, and therefore he was crowned with laurel to display this quality. Raphael is crowning the head of Il Perugino, who was his teacher and a reader of the Bible from which he was inspired. To the right of Perugino there is a head with a small part of the face. This is Raphael himself, presented here as a young student, very much dependent on his master. Here is the very symbol of the modesty that governed Raphael's artistic life. Raphael's bent head is an act of dignified subservience to Perugino and to the book from which Perugino gets his wisdom. At the same time, by putting his left hand on Perugino's left shoulder and his right hand on the top right of the book, he shows his desire to receive this knowledge.

To the right of the figure of Jesus is the figure of John, standing by himself. He stands alone as the most beloved apostle and the one who gives us the most esoteric knowledge of Christianity. By identifying the four apostles surrounding Jesus, it becomes obvious that the most prominent figure on the steps, and separate from the others, is Paul.

This group also contains portraits of Jesus at different stages of development – one as an adult and two as a child – as well as a portrait of Mary. One portrait of Jesus is the child Jesus from the Gospel of Matthew (Figure 7-12) and the other is the Luke Jesus child at the time of the temple incident (Figure 7-8). To understand these images we must be aware of the mystery of the two Jesus children.

Matthew's Gospel begins with the genealogy of one of the Jesus children, showing that he is a descendant of kings and therefore entitled to the Israelite kingdom. The magi, guided by star lore, come to bring him gifts of gold, frankincense, and myrrh. Gold is the symbol of thinking, Frankincense symbolizes the pity and compassion pervading feeling, and myrrh is the power of the will.

Below the messenger on the left is an old man with a green cap. This is Joseph, father of the Jesus child referred to in the Gospel of Matthew. Below him is an infant, the Matthew Jesus, sitting on a pedestal holding a book. The child and book, positioned at the base of the arch which encompasses the *School of Athens,* indicate that Christian knowledge is at the base of the School and of all knowledge in the Western world. The child has obtained early spiritual maturity and is therefore able to sacrifice himself. According to Steiner's indications, he is a leader who carries within himself the wisdom of many lives, the impulses of the early leaders of humankind, and insights concerning the mysteries of the Sun, stars and Earth.

On the right side of the pedestal is the other Jesus child at the age of twelve, the time of the temple episode described in Luke's Gospel. This Jesus child carries within himself aspects of the original soul of humanity; therefore, it could be said that he is the Son of God, ready to become a human son. There is no recorded history from the birth of this Jesus to the incident at the temple.

The incident at the temple helps us to inwardly understand the mystery of the two Jesus children. As Rudolf Steiner explained, this event brings about a profound change in both children. The Luke Jesus at the temple expands and opens his being and makes himself capable of receiving the Matthew Jesus' soul, thereby becoming a complete ego. Mary, as the mother of the Luke Jesus, sees the change in him, but she is not able to comprehend it. Her destiny is fulfilled and she dies early. It is worthwhile to note that each Mary, painted by Raphael in his many works, has the countenance of a woman in her teens, which portrays her purity. The orphaned Luke Jesus is adopted by the Matthew Mary, who is older and already has six children of her own. She is painted right below the Luke Jesus and next to the pedestal. Her head is covered with a green shawl, embroidered in gold. Curly golden hair streams from under this cap and rests on her red garment, which is barely visible. Her goddess-like characteristics are those of a wise woman, mature and cognizant of the cosmos. This is the divine aspect of woman, of Mary, known as Sophia. She was the one who understood the change as indicated by her serene face and by her left hand, placed between the head and the shoulder of the two figures in front of her. Her hand has the thumb and index finger extended, indicating the number two. This is a confirmation of the esoteric event of the two Jesus children.

Next to Luke is the head of an angel-like figure, which recalls Leonardo's *Annunciation* and *Madonna of the Rocks* angels. This figure's face is directed toward Mary, but he is looking at Luke. With his left hand he is holding a tablet with the title "epogdoon," meaning "full tone." This tablet contains the human understanding of cosmic relationships understood through music and arithmetic ratios. Below this title there are several U-shapes, the largest U, encompassing all the others is the diapason, one octave. The single smaller U is the diapente, a quinte. The smallest U is the diatesseron, a quarte. The upper end of the U shapes shows the dividing of the string, which produces these intervals. The octave 6:12, the quinte 6:9 and 8:12, the quarte 6:8 and 9:12. Below this picture of vibrations is the tetractys. The numbers one to four in Roman numerals (I, II, III, IV) total the sum of ten (X. Raphael again uses polarity within the composition by placing Music and Arithmetic on the left side and Geometry and Astronomy on the right side within the group in the foreground, dividing the Quadrivium of the seven Liberal Arts practiced in the Middle Ages.

The heel and ankle of a right foot are visible on the left-hand side of the tablet. This foot belongs to the figure wrapped in white. White stands for earthly purity and for the image of light. The garment is embroidered with gold, which stands for the splendor of light; therefore, we can say that this figure bears purity and splendor of light, divine wisdom. He has golden curly hair which frames his oval face elliptically, symbolic of eternity. This is the adult Jesus. His posture and hand held over his heart emphasize that he is the carrier of love.

The figure next to Jesus is John with his head leaning towards Jesus' bosom and with his body moving away from Jesus. He is holding an open book, pointing with his hand, as if wanting to show what he has written. His book is resting on his left thigh. His left foot is resting on a pedestal while his right foot is firmly grounded. This figure is the only one, with the exception of Plato, to have three-colored garments. John is given the three primary colors, a pictorial full tone. The lower part of this garment is red, which is then turned inside out and becomes blue over his shoulder. This unusual garment is embroidered in gold. The blue over his shoulders covers a yellow shirt. Placed next to the white garments of Jesus, these colors portray the connection of John to Jesus as the manifestation of light from the spiritual world in its transition from white to the primary colors. He stands alone with a graceful gesture with his head in the past and his limbs in the future. The figure of John the Evangelist concludes the intimate family of Jesus.

On the right hand side a virtual triangle, similar to the one on the left, is made by the hypotenuse starting at the exiting messenger and going to Paul (Figure 6-C ⟶ B). Here the individuals are grouped in schools or absorbed in themselves. The foreground group of five figures has at its center a bald man's head. This man is bent over a tablet and uses a compass to demonstrate his thinking to a group of students who interact with each other. This group is separated from Diogenes, not only by a space, but also by a figure who is turned toward the inside of the school. The outer lines of the left hand delineate an empty space between Diogenes and this school. There is no connection or interaction between him and the school; the outermost figures are turning their backs on him. Not all schools, then, are affected by Diogenes' principle of knowledge for knowledge's sake – selfishness.

The students represent four stages of learning. The first one, closest to the ground and to the master, is the beginner; he shows the intensity needed to perceive what the master is communicating. The figure above has the right hand on the shoulder of the lower figure and with his left hand he is gesturing as if arguing what has been communicated. His finger is at the head level of the figure next to him pointing directly to the mental process of learning. The third student, kneeling to his right, is pointing down to the tablet and looking up to his fellow student on his left-hand side as if asking, "What is it that you see that I don't?" The fourth figure with open arms and serene face is the one who has comprehended the master's communication.

Next to this group of four students and one master is another group of four adults. Of this group, two are prominent because of their garments and the other two, by contrast, are almost fading into the background. Of the two prominent figures, one with his back toward the beholder is holding a globe of the earth, and another figure opposite him, is gently holding with the tips of his fingers a globe of stars. Here we have earthly and cosmic wisdom. Earthly wisdom is held by the faceless kingly figure. This figure has a crown and rich garments embroidered in gold. He stands firmly on one foot while he lifts the other one, as if in the process of moving onward. His golden and blue garment indicates a soul full of cognition. The facelessness of this crowned and richly-dressed figure indicates Raphael's desire to represent an unusual, unidentifiable spiritual entity. It is fair to assume that this is a graphic representation of Zarathustra.

The other figure has an ancient, priestly countenance. He is bearded and his eyes express serenity derived from a detached wisdom. He is Melchizedek, a high priest who has a particular relationship to Christianity and brings the wisdom of the stars to humanity. Both figures are looking toward the other two figures standing below the arc, which encompasses the whole school. Those two figures are Raphael and his predecessor, Giovanni Pazzi, also known as Sodoma, six years older than Raphael, who recognized Raphael's genius. Through this friendship Raphael became aware of his own abilities to translate earthly and cosmic wisdom into the pictorial representation seen here as Zarathustra and Melchizedek. However, Raphael was so intimately connected to Sodoma that he had to isolate himself from his influence in order to nurture his own creative impulse. In this vein, Raphael built a brick wall to cover Sodoma's frescos in order to paint. On the left-hand side we saw Raphael obliging his master; here we see him on equal footing with leaders of humankind.

Right above this group there is a figure whose right arm is almost outside the painting and who is looking backwards, as he is carrying on the impulse generated by the incoming messenger on the left side. This figure indicates that knowledge imbued with Christianity will be carried on into the future. This figure's left hand is directly above Raphael's cap, as if acknowledging the major contribution Raphael makes to carry this impulse into the future. We can deduce that the purpose of knowledge, as depicted in the work of Raphael, is always evolving. Knowledge is perpetually being transformed for understanding today and then passed into the future for further investigation and refinement, as well as adaptation to the needs of the time.

The unique technique that Raphael uses on many occasions is seen in the out-rushing figure and in John the Evangelist. Each figure bends the head backwards into the past, while the limbs are directed to the future, and the whole body is in the present. From the esoteric knowledge communicated by Rudolf Steiner we know that the head is formed from impulses, which lived in the limbs in the past reincarnation. The limbs of this incarnation will form the head in the future incarnation.

In contrast to the *Disputa* where everything was pointing toward a cosmic activity, here the lines of time indicate the evolution of human investigations, and the slightly downward perspective indicates that the process of thinking is housed in the brain and the brain is within the skull. In the *Disputa* the perspective lines are rising toward a spiritual world. In the *School of Athens* the lines in the foreground create a downward movement, shown by the downward triangle (Figure 6-A–B–C). The vaults also create a downward movement to the human realm rather than leading to the spiritual world as in the *Disputa.* The heavens are seen between the vaults, but the human realm is principally enclosed.

The *School of Athens* stands as a counterpoint to the *Disputa.* Therefore it is no coincidence that the paintings are actually situated opposite each other. In the *Disputa* all activities of humankind are directed toward the cosmos, while here the activities of humankind are directed to the understanding of our very own selves through art, science, philosophy. All these activities made available to humankind take place in time, showing the development of consciousness, and are imbued with the Divine Love incarnated through the Christ impulse.

The triangle to the left of the viewer, into which the Christian impulse is painted, stands in counterpoint to the one on the right, where wisdom is depicted in the form of schools. The difference between these groups is accentuated by the difference between their interactions within each group – the figures within the Christ group look to one another for understanding, whereas the figures within the school on the right look up to a teacher so that the intent in their spirits is brought to conscious knowledge. These two triangles break the symbolic time line – the abscissae – and this could be considered as musical notes bringing harmony to consciousness.

The figures drawn above the horizontal lines are the major emphasis of this painting, as if Raphael wanted to indicate that all the activities are inscribed in earthly time; therefore they are finite. Both parts are of equal value, of equal importance. Each sees the world in a different way; however, complete thinking is developed only through their collaboration. Does not Plato talk about nature in his work *Timaeus*? Does not Aristotle carry *Ethics* in his hand? Is not Apollo god of the sun and Athena goddess of wisdom? In the true dialectic, oppositions become one. Only through both the sciences and philosophical disciplines, can the temple of wisdom be built.

The Apollonian feminine principle of the arts is to the left; the Athenian masculine element of the sciences is to the right. Combining the Platonic and Aristotelian modes of thinking brings balance.

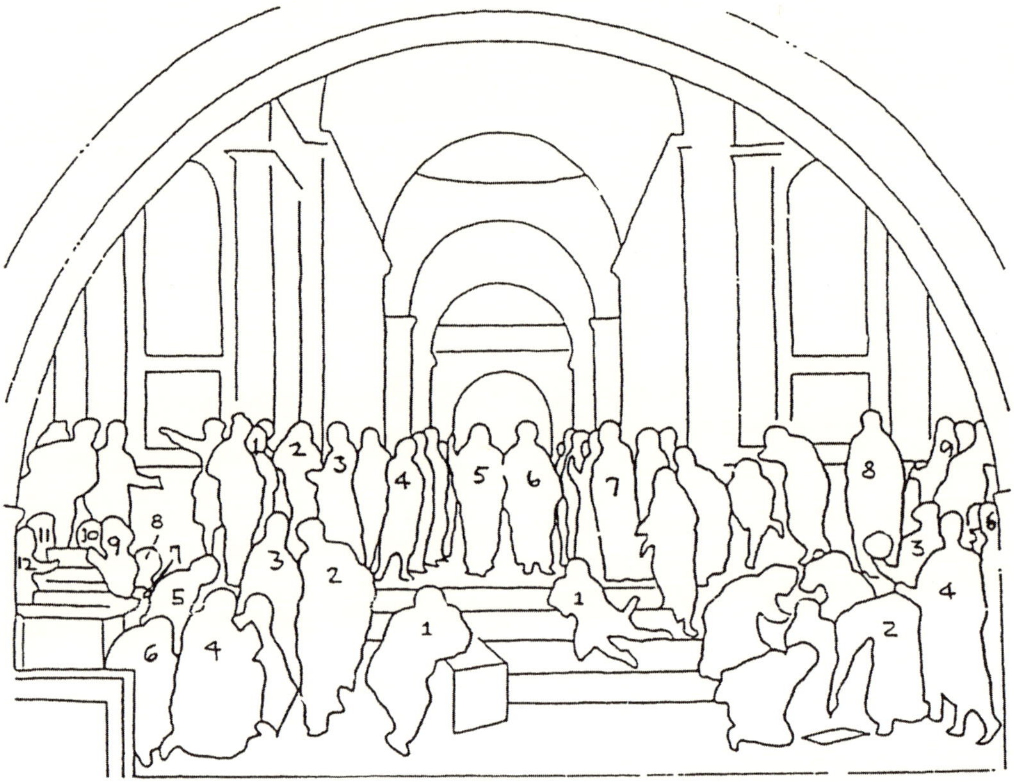

Figure 7

Identities Attributed by Citics to Figures in the *School of Athens*

Lower left

1. Paul
2. John the Evangelist
3. Christ
4. Mark
5. Luke
6. Matthew
7. Mary
8. The Luke portrayal of Jesus at the time of the Temple incident
9. Il Perugino
10. Raphael as a child
11. Joseph
12. The infant Jesus from the Gospel of Matthew

Lower Right

1. Diogenes
2. Identified as Euclid or Archimedes or Pythagoras.
3. Melchizedek
4. Zarathustra
5. Raphael
6. Giovanni Pazzi, also known as Sodoma, friend of Raphael.

Upper Figures

1. Pericles, uncle of Alkibiades; he has covered his deformed skull with a hat. Pericles recognized the potential of Alkibiades; he is painted as if leaning on Alkibiades.
2. Alkibiades, very obedient to Socrates' influence, became a mentor and a member of the enlightenment movement.
3. Socrates
4. Alexander the Great
5. Plato
6. Aristotle
7. Xenophon of Colophaus, also known as Xenophon from Ilea in southern Italy
8. Anaxagoras who was concerned with the archetypal building blocks of the universe
9. Oedipus painted with a green hooded cloak guides himself with a wooden staff.

The Transfiguration

Shortly before he died, Raphael received a commission for two paintings. He started the first one, the *Transfiguration,* on canvas, but never finished it. His pupils worked on the painting after his death. A few biographers claim that this painting accompanied Raphael's funeral procession to the Pantheon where he was entombed. Others claim that it was placed at the head of his deathbed.

At first glance the predominant part of the painting is the top, which is noticeably luminous and requires little effort by the viewer to recognize the harmonious composition of the figures painted within a circle. Because of the different sizes of the figures, however, their spatial distribution is ambiguous. Where does Christ float, in front of or behind the apostles? Is the light coming from the back as radiation from a central point, or is it a diffused light?

From the left-hand side of the painting, light falls on the Christ, but the light falling on the two figures on each side of him comes from the Christ himself.

The three figures strewn on the ground, with the two just outside the circle, receive light as if it is coming from beyond the Christ.

There seems to be some distance between Christ and the clouds, but the gray value of the clouds and of Christ's foot makes one wonder if he is really touching the clouds.

All this may be interpreted to mean that the laws of physical reality have been purposely abandoned and that, in this context, physical laws are infused with spiritual ones. The underlying composition, when fully comprehended, is vital to an understanding of what Raphael is conveying, something far beyond the visual depiction of a historical or Biblical event. However, we will find that the composition of this painting elucidates the wisdom that operated through Raphael.

The composition of lower part of the painting, which depicts a child in a fit of epilepesy, is in stark contrast to the upper portion; seeming, at first glance, to be only an agglomeration of figures pointing at one another with dramatic gestures and lacking any coherence.

In fact, this lower part of the *Transfiguration* has caused many critics to disregard the painting as one of the worst attempts at composition ever done by a painter. Italians have ignored it and have often treated it with scorn. American critics have used it as an example of miscarriage in composition.

However, this painting actually reveals a rich parallel in combining the epileptic's episode with Christ's transfiguration. I will use a series of diagrams to demonstrate the layers of Raphael's composition that contribute to the full realization of the work.

The virtual circle created by the figures that are painted at the top of the *Transfiguration* is obvious.

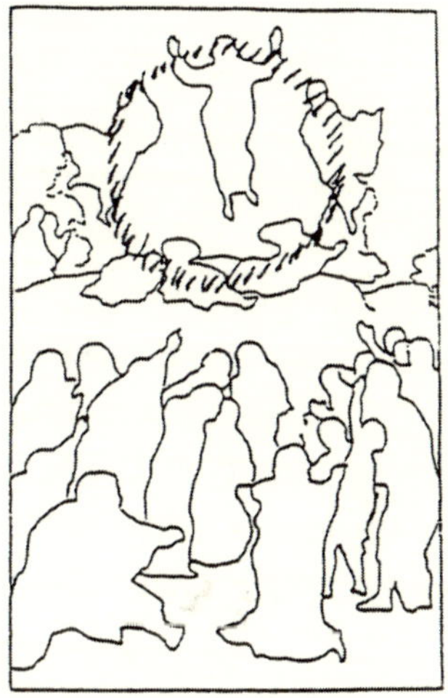

The lower circle is subtle.

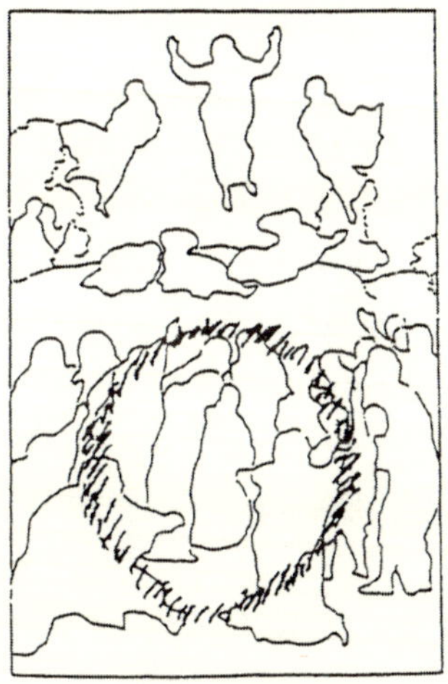

By drawing a line starting at the first of the two figures on the far left of the upper section of the painting, and carrying this line across the second figure and to the third one, the line reaches the right hand of the Christ. From there the line goes through the fifth figure and onto the figures sprawled on the ground. This line transforms the circle into a spiral.

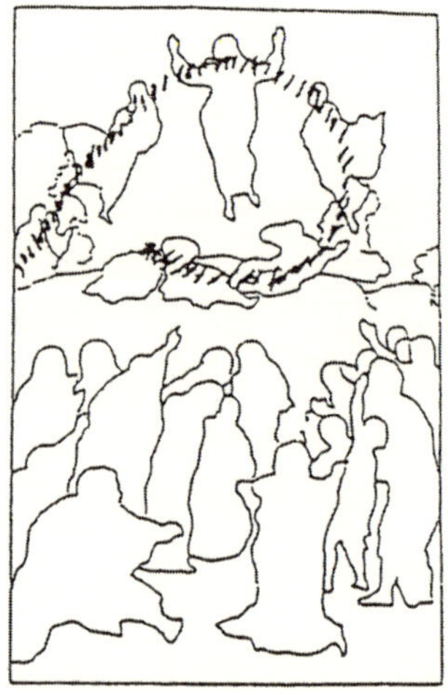

On the lower portion, the line starts at the landscape painted on the right. The first figure coming from the landscape brings the line to the epileptic. From there the line goes to the kneeling figure and to the gesturing apostles and concludes with the apostle pointing at the epileptic. The lower circle has also become a spiral.

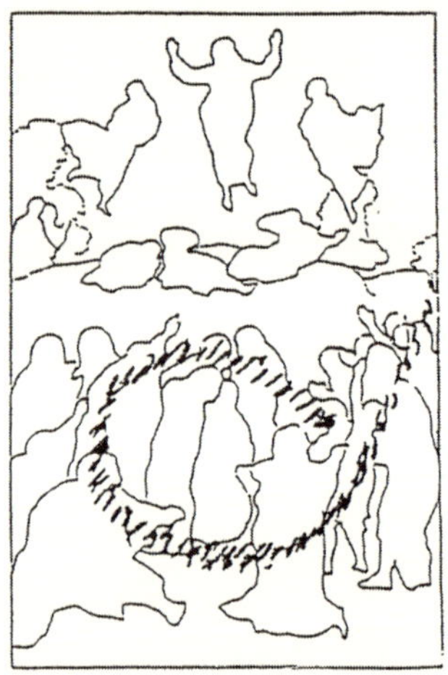

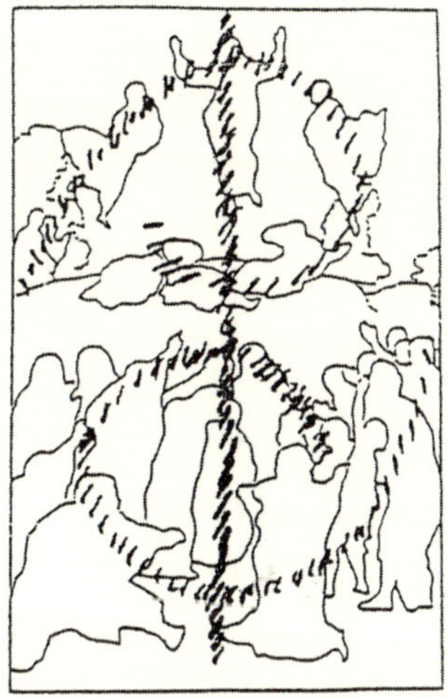

The top and bottom spirals are spinning around an axis and in an opposite direction.

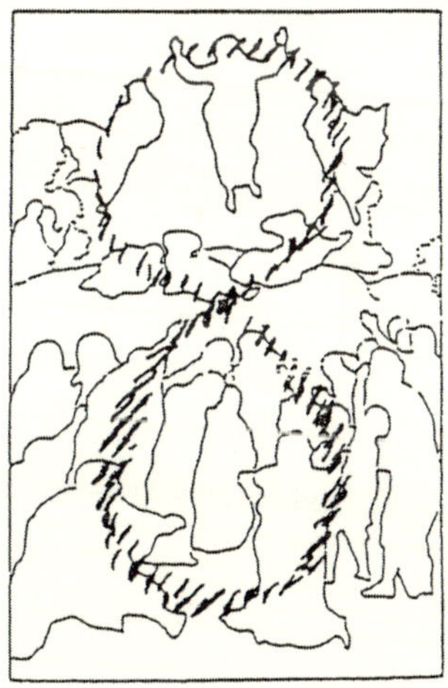

From what has been said it is an easy task to visualize how the two circles with the two spirals can be metamorphosed into a Cassini lemniscate.

The Cassini lemniscate can be inscribed within the oval, which is embracing the lower and upper part of the painting.

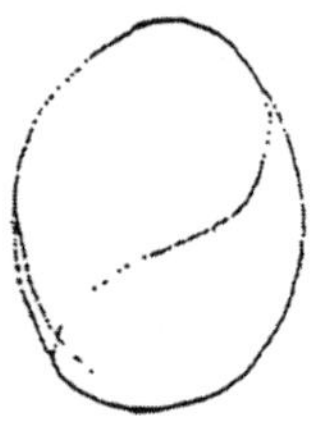

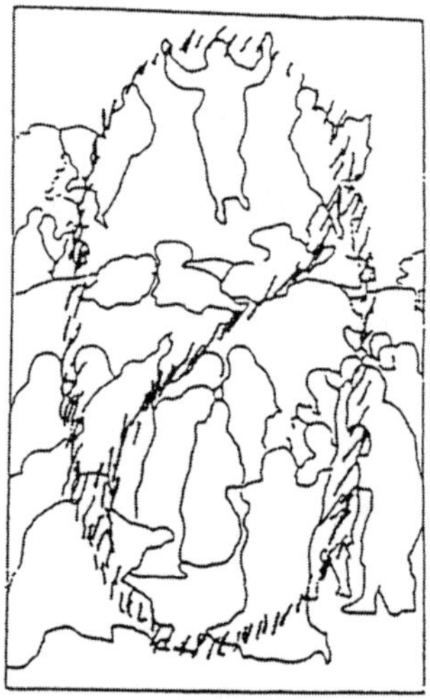

The Jesus figure repeats these composition themes. His raised arms, his head and the halo of his floating garments can be inscribed with Cassini lemniscates.

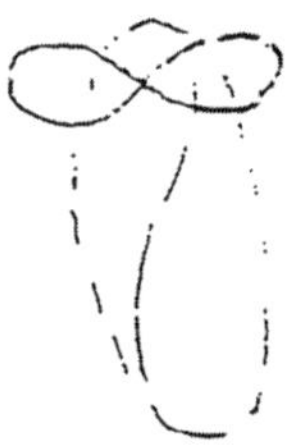

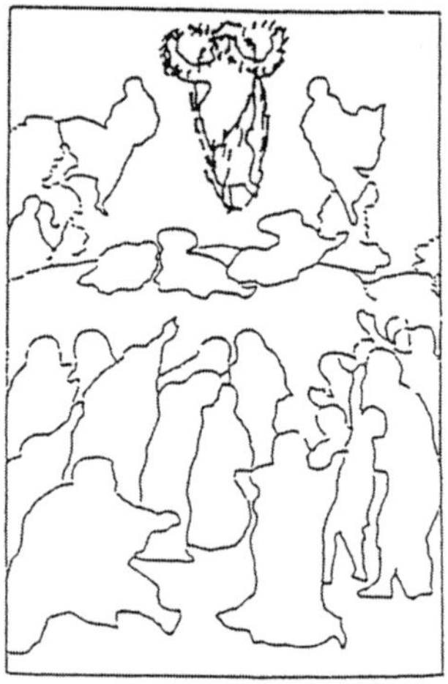

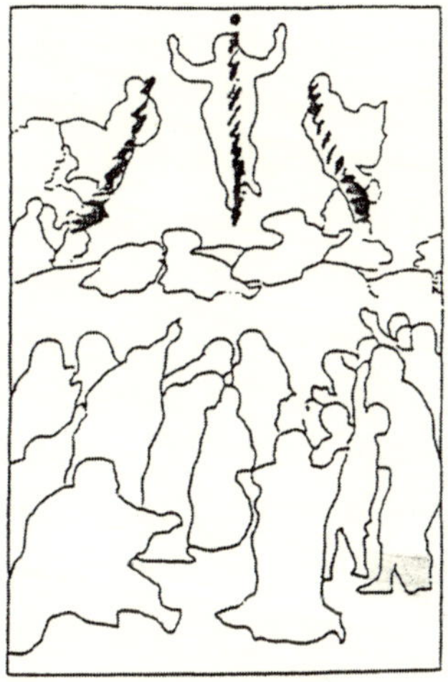

We learned from the Gospels of Matthew and Mark that Jesus went to the mountain with his three chosen apostles. There he revealed to them his spiritual splendor.

Raphael, by painting Elijah and Moses leaning toward the Jesus, indicates that their spiritual activity was necessary for the Jesus to achieve his splendor.

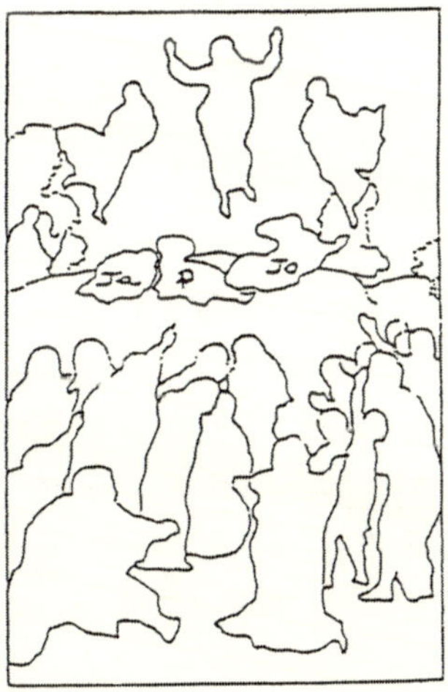

Below these figures, John with his right hand holds his head and shields his eyes as if unable to withstand the intensity of the light from above (Jo). The emphasis on the head signifies John's spiritual concentration: *Thinking*. Next to John is Peter lying on his left side (P). He is painted with a particular emphasis on his chest, indicating *Feeling*. In the *Disputa* Peter is painted with this chest emphasis. Next to Peter, James with folded arms and legs and praying hands, directs his attention to the earth (Ja). The emphasis on his hips indicates that he represents *Will.*

On the left side of James are two kneeling figures gazing at the Christ. The one, strongly lighted, has his left hand open and aimed toward the light while his right hand is directed toward the earth. This figure, with his open, serene face, has been identified as Felicitus, the martyr, whose name means the happy one. The garments of Felicitus, painted in subdued mystical color, have strong vertical folds, indicating a balance between the physical and spiritual realms.

His companion Agapitus, the loved one, is also a martyr. He is portrayed as a counterpoint to Felicitus through color and gesture. His hands raised in prayer show his humility; he is ready to sacrifice himself. Felicitus and Agapitus are commemorated on August 6, the date of the Transfiguration.

These two figures depict two ways of developing consciousness. Felicitus, through the gesture of his hands—his left hand opened toward the Christ while his right is open toward the earth—shows that he is developing knowledge of the spiritual as well as of the physical. He achieves this experience through contemplation. Agapitus, by closing his hands over his chest, shows the on-going development of his inner self. Each represents a soul activity leading to the Christ.

By painting these two martyrs outside the circle in these particular attitudes, Raphael is indicating that contemplation and sacrifice can develop a consciousness, which can bring one to a direct experience of the transfigured Christ and of the Christian impulse. The martyrs are at the same level as the three apostles, but markedly outside their circle of light, showing that this new process must also transform the soul activities represented by the three apostles in order to be intimately experienced. Every human being can become conscious of the Christ through the activities of thinking, feeling and willing. These three spiritual faculties, living in each and every human being, are the vessels in which the Christ can reside and through which he reveals himself.

At first glance, the strong gesticulations of the various figures in the lower half of the painting distracts the viewer from the main composition mentioned previously. A closer look will reveal an organization that relates to the upper portion of the painting, yielding a cohesive whole.

On the right-hand side, a group of figures enters the scene from a background of nature. This group comes from farm communities, and the figures are painted predominantly in green and blue. The central figure is the child in a fit of epilepsy. The dramatic gesture of his right hand going up and his left hand going down can be understood from the description Rudolf Steiner gave for the Eurythmy[1]

1. For an introduction to the principles and practice of the movement art of Eurythmy founded by Rudolf Steiner see *Eurythmy: Rhythm, Dance and Soul,* Thomas Poplawski, Hudson, NY: Anthroposophic Press, 1998.

movement of the vowel sound "i" ("ee"), which is the soul gesture of the I: the Ego. In this case, showing the trauma of the child's soul through the intense contortion of his muscles and splayed fingers. The facial expression of the father, who is grasping his child, shows that while he sees the activity around him he does not comprehend it. His foot is firmly on the ground, displaying his simple, direct approach to the world. The father is the simplest form of stupor without mental struggle.

Counterpoint to the father is Judas who is being directed to the child by the pointing man. Judas' facial expression displays a mental struggle to comprehend what is happening to the child. Judas and the father represent intellectual labor and simple awe. On the left-hand side of the child is a kneeling woman, separated from him by a blue cloak. With her right hand she points to the child's heart while she looks to the left. Her left arm comes forward in what seems to be a gesture of both defense and comprehension. Light illuminates her left side from the hair to the knee, giving emphasis to the female principal. The intensity of this light is similar to the one used on the epileptic child.

At first, this figure seems to lack integration within the whole framework of this painting. She stands out in the lower part of the painting because of her coiffed hair, determined and firm gaze, and kneeling position. Her foot and toes are poised as if ready to leap into action. Raphael has placed her outside the center of the composition in order to emphasize her philosophical meaning rather than her physical importance to the work of art.

Taking all of the above into account, and giving special consideration to her beautifully combed hair with braided tresses wound onto each other, we can suggest that this figure is Sophia, the traditional representation of wisdom. The way Sophia is painted gives her awareness, which, lighted by the solar quality of Christ, does not allow conjecture, speculation, or poor reasoning. She represents the highest form of knowledge.

To the left of Sophia is the apostle Matthew, who is sitting on a tree trunk that projects over water. He is elevated, raised from the earth. On this precarious foundation the apostle is holding a book and his foot is not touching the ground. The apostle's gesture indicates that traditional knowledge, symbolized by the book, is insufficient for comprehending the events. His gesture of reaching toward Sophia shows that his understanding of the Christ comes through the mediation of Sophia, the pursuit of wisdom. Above him an apostle looks at the child and gestures towards Christ, emphasizing the connection between the upper and lower worlds.

To the right of this gesturing apostle and at the center of the lower half, is a group of four figures. A young man and an older man are staring in bewildered curiosity at the child. Above these two an apostle is pointing out the child to the figure on his right, Judas, who shows great stress from trying to understand the event.

Judas, surrounded by three individuals, is at the physical center of the painting. His eyes are closed to slits as if in an intellectual effort. His tense and obtuse attention follows the clear gesture of the arm and hand of the individual on his left who points at the epileptic. The placement of Judas at the center of the composition emphasizes the judging quality of the intellect. The figure that questions Judas, perhaps Simon the Cananaean, is calling upon Judas to understand the event. Judas' inability to comprehend the "lunar" affliction of epilepsy leads to his inability to comprehend what Steiner calls the Solar Spirit, the incarnated Jesus Christ. This inability to understand the relationship between the physical and spiritual prevents him from forming a mental picture of good and evil, leading him to error. Raphael's skills are at the very best in depicting Judas' troubled soul. This portraiture of the inability to form judgment is emphasized by the clear, fully-lighted figure gesturing on Judas's right, who has been named Bartholomew.

Below Judas, a young man looks with curiosity at the epileptic, as if he were an unusual specimen. To the left of this young man is a man with extended hands, who is both attracted to the epileptic and defending himself from comprehending the event. His particularly-highlighted hand indicates that this individual's understanding is limited to what he touches – Thomas the Doubter. This group at the physical center of the canvas, with Judas at the very center, would indicate individuals with reserved concern about the epileptic.

On the same level as Judas, on the opposite side of Bartholemew, are two figures so absorbed in themselves that they are unconcerned with what is happening around them. In one way or another, these six figures are unable to comprehend the spiritual climate above them or understand the spiritual reflection manifested in the child. They live with attitudes similar to that of Judas. Their self-centeredness emphasizes the action portrayed by the three other figures, two pointing up to the Christ and the other reaching toward Sophia.

It is important here to note that Raphael, as well as many other Renaissance painters, used the landscape as a primary and integral part of the artist's philosophical communication instead of as a secondary or decorative element.

The two martyrs at the top left of the painting are placed in a background of trees, indicating that they have transformed their natural pattern of life through meditation and sacrifice, and therefore were able to have a direct comprehension of the transfiguration of Christ. In contrast to the martyrs, at the opposite lower side, the group of farmers is not capable of similar comprehension because their destiny at the time of this event is to remain within the natural environment. The relationship of the Christ to the epileptic is beyond their ordinary life experience and their souls are not as yet attuned to what is happening.

The dynamic character of this lower fragmented circle is heightened by the arrangement of colors used to paint the figures. The left side is predominantly red while the right side is blue. The dramatic up-swinging gesture of the two figures on the left, pointing to the event on the mountain, counterbalances Sophia's horizontal gesture. The standing apostle dominates the scene because of his large red garment. This intense red makes the group of four figures to the right and the two to the left subdued, even though they are painted against a very dark background.

With careful analysis of this painting we can recognize the wisdom that operated through Raphael. His artistic talent allowed him to transcend the physical qualities of his figures. He did not copy onto the canvas a mere model posed in a particular attitude. Through the activity of sketching models, he internalized their bearing. When he faced the space designated for his figures, he did not look at the physical models, but at the memory of the models he had acquired through sketches. Therefore, the physical models became pictorial realities, fitting the space at their disposal with attitudes and gestures needed to reveal his intuition.

When Raphael was asked where he found the beautiful models he used for his Madonnas, he replied that if he couldn't find one he invented what he needed. By looking in his memory he found a source for an archetypal beauty that was similar to the inspiring source used by Greek artists.

Only through this artistic discipline could the figures of Jesus Christ, Elijah and Moses come into being as they did. These figures are free, liberated from any physical weight. The Christ figure is expanding and ascending toward spatial heights and becomes the axis, the power that attracts Elijah on the left and Moses on the right. These three figures are pictorially interdependent and their garments emphasize the free interpenetration of the spiritual world, in contrast to the three apostles on the mountain with their determined gestures.

Within the overall composition, four basic compositional structures are overlaid upon each other; the upper space is dominated by the Christ figure whose gestures harmonize with the rest of the space around Him.

The lower space, with its dramatically gesturing figures, gives at first glance the impression of chaos, but here Sophia is standing as the counterpoint to the figure of the Christ. With her erect torso, and head, arm and feet positions, Sophia is ready to sprint into action so as to bring to order the disarray around the epileptic child and bring into consciousness his relationship to the Christ.

Sophia's placement in the foreground of the painting accentuates her significance. Geometrically she is almost opposite to Jesus; however she relinquishes the focus of the center with her gesture towards the epileptic who becomes the philosophical focal point in the lower part of this painting.

Sophia's gesture toward the epileptic is complemented by the gesture of the red-robed apostle, whose arm and finger points to the upper level, producing an upward movement. However, the disciple who points at the child offsets this movement. This contrapuntal gesturing indicates that whatever is making this child a lunatic is beyond the capabilities of anyone present to reckon with and requires a power which only Jesus Christ has.

It is worth mentioning that Rudolf Steiner in his lecture of June 28, 1914 entitled "A New Conception of Architecture,"[2] in made a didactic demonstration of how the circle, hyperbola, ellipse, and Cassini lemniscate affect our soul.

In *The Transfiguration,* the circle is obvious, the hyperbola is partially hidden, and the ellipse and Cassini lemniscate are hidden. However, as soon as we form a mental picture of these hidden geometrical forms, we can understand the wisdom underlying this painting and recognize that the composition is not nonsensical or chaotic at all, but is composed to convey a very specific meaning both philosophically and visually. This can be summarized in the following way:

Upper Half

2. *Architecture as a Synthesis of the Arts,* ed. Christian Thal-Jantzen, London: Rudolf Steiner Press, 1999.

Metamorphosis of the Geometrical Elements of *The Transfiguration*

With regard to form and space distribution of the figures we have division and symmetry.

This is the BODY.

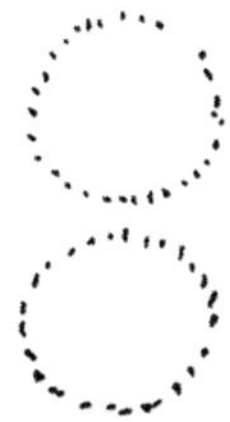

With regard the figures' gestures we have polarity and dynamism.

This is LIFE.

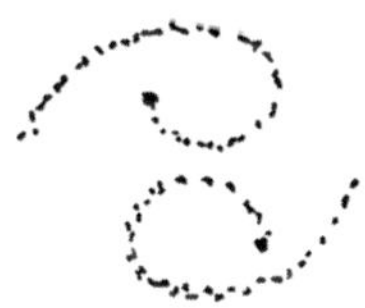

With regard to the figures' expressions we have reunion and synthesis.

This is SOUL.

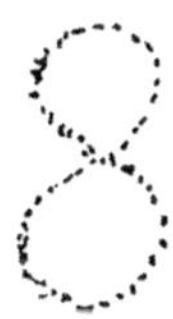

With regard to the idea we have concentration, unity and totality.

This is SPIRIT.

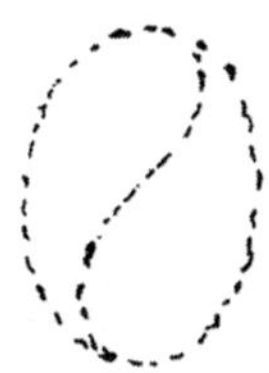

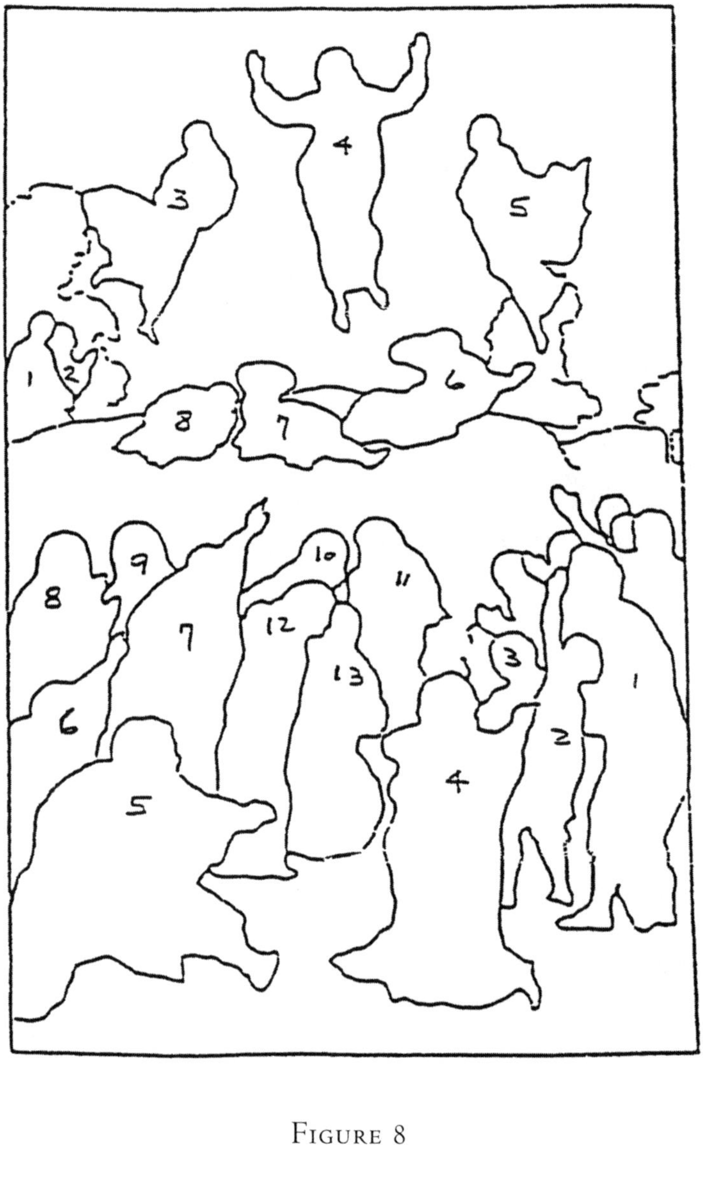

Figure 8

Identities Attributed by Critics to Figures in the *Transfiguration*

1. Felicitus
2. Agapitus
3. Elijah
4. Jesus
5. Moses
6. John
7. Peter
8. James the Greater

Lower Half

1. Father of epileptic child
2. Epileptic child
3. Mother of epileptic child
4. Sophia
5. Matthew
6. Philip, friend of Bartholomew
7. Bartholomew
8. Andrew
9. Thaddeus
10. Judas
11. Simon the Cananaean, friend of Judas
12. James the Lesser, son of Alphaeus
13. Thomas

Final Comments

DURING MY EXPLORATION of Raphael's three paintings I have become more and more aware that, while the advent of Christianity is the main theme of these paintings, Raphael places this advent not only within the context of a religious world concept, but within the development of knowledge: The School of Athens.

Christianity is a spiritual activity that incarnated in Palestine and has generally been interpreted mainly as a religious impulse. This religious impulse lived in other parts of the world but incarnated in Palestine in the form of Christianity for the needs of the particular segment of humanity that was to incarnate in the West, mainly in Europe. I cannot help but think that Christianity, as seen consciously or unconsciously by Raphael, came to help humans become aware of their individuality.

It seems obvious that the Christian impulse had to develop with the help of Rome. I understand that the Romans were the first to adopt testamentary laws, which allow an individual to designate his or her heirs, and for those heirs to receive what goods the deceased leaves behind.

In the *Transfiguration,* Raphael combines two events as they are described in the New Testament into one painting, and he painted these events on a geometrical form – the figure eight, the symbol of infinity – known in the West as the Cassini lemniscate and in the East as the Yin and Yang.

This brings me to ask if Raphael's intuition operated in such a way as to give us a visual representation of a spiritual event, showing the metamorphosis of universal spiritual activity which is necessary for the future development of humanity; development not only in a religious sense, but the total awareness of how spiritual activities can manifest physically.

I cannot help but imagine at this time in my long life that the physical aspects of our lives and our surroundings are translations of spiritual activities into concrete appearances. Whether we are able to recognize this or not depends on the collective and individual spiritual organization of a particular period of our lives.

Resources

Becherucci, L. *Raphael.* New York: Harrison House, 1969. (Ignores Raphael's compositions.)

Canaday, J. *Seminars of Art.* Metropolitan Museum of Art. (Uses Raphael's *Transfiguration* as an example of the worst of compositional efforts.)

Krause-Zimmer, Hella. *Die Zwe: Jesuslenaben in der Gildenden Kunst.* Stuttgart: Verlag Freies Geistesleben, 1964.

Marangoni. (Italian critic, whose book became a text for Italian school use, disregards *The Transfiguration* as a failed attempt at composition.)

Serra, L. *Raffaelo.* (Similar attitude as above, but less adamant.)

Other sources whose authors give particular attention to the qualities of Raphael's paintings:

Oberhuber, Konrad. "Raphael's Transfiguration und Polaritat und Synthese" in *Raphael's Schule von Athen.*

—. *A Masterpiece Close-up: The Transfiguration by Raphael.* Cambridge, Mass.: Fogg Art Museum, 1980.

Scheck, Hanns. *Raphael's geistige Mission am Beispiel seiner "Stanza Segnature."*
Steiner, Rudolf. Lectures on Raphael.
Ytter, Herald Falk. *Raphael's Christologie: Disputa und Schule von Athen.*

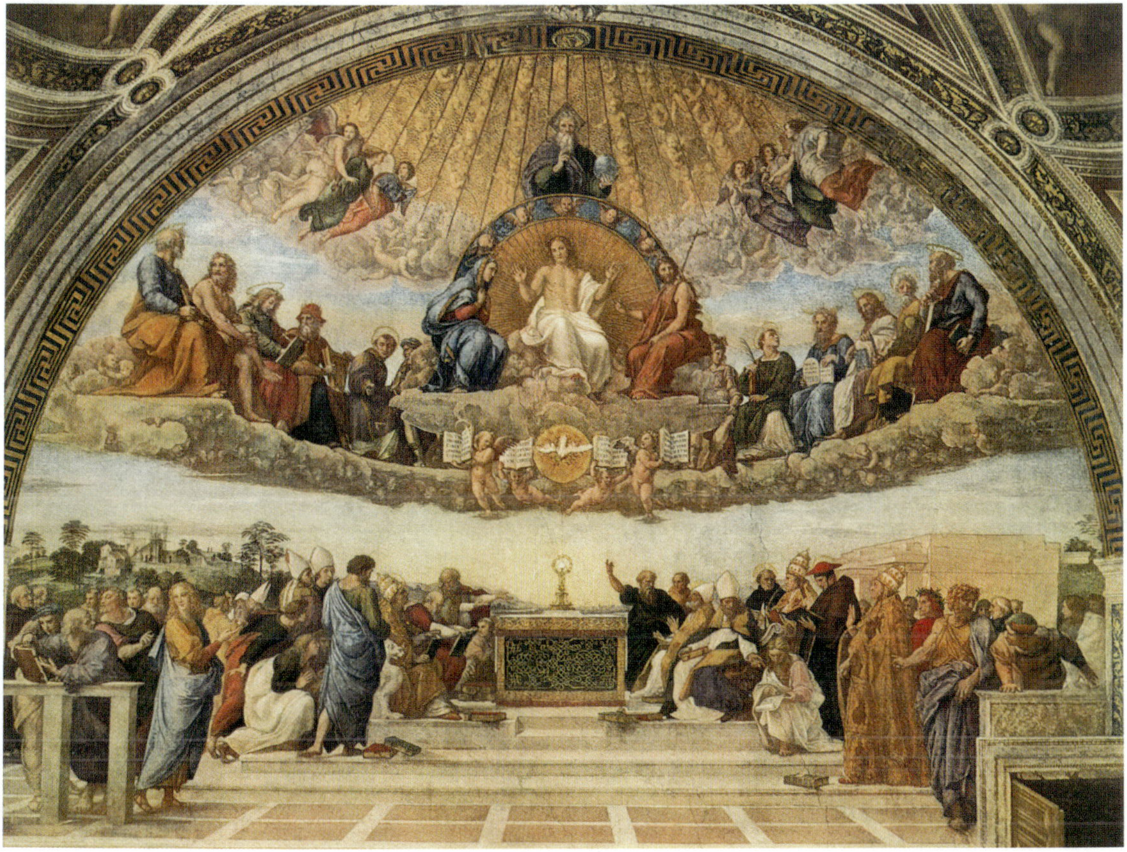

The Disputa [La Disputa] 1510-11
Fresco. Stanza della Signatura, Vatican, Rome.

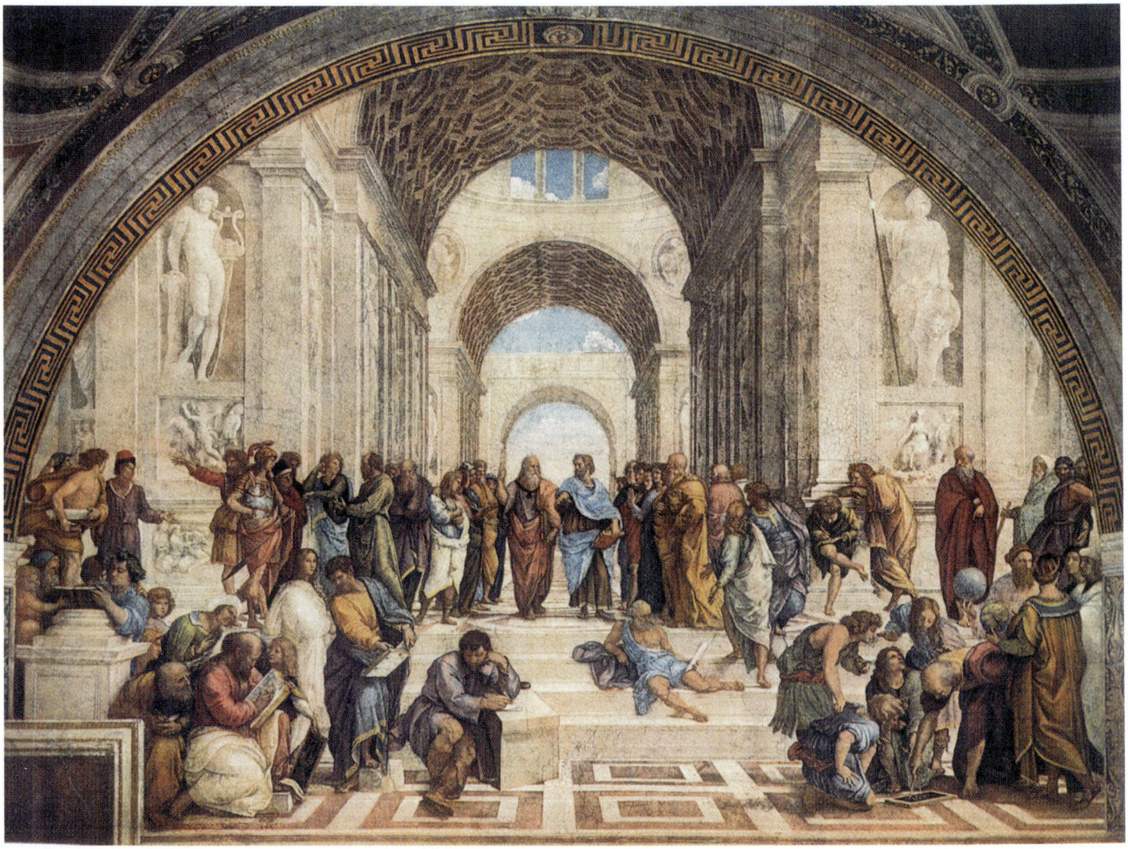

The School of Athens [La Scuola di Atena] 1509-10
Fresco. Stanza della Signatura, Vatican, Rome.

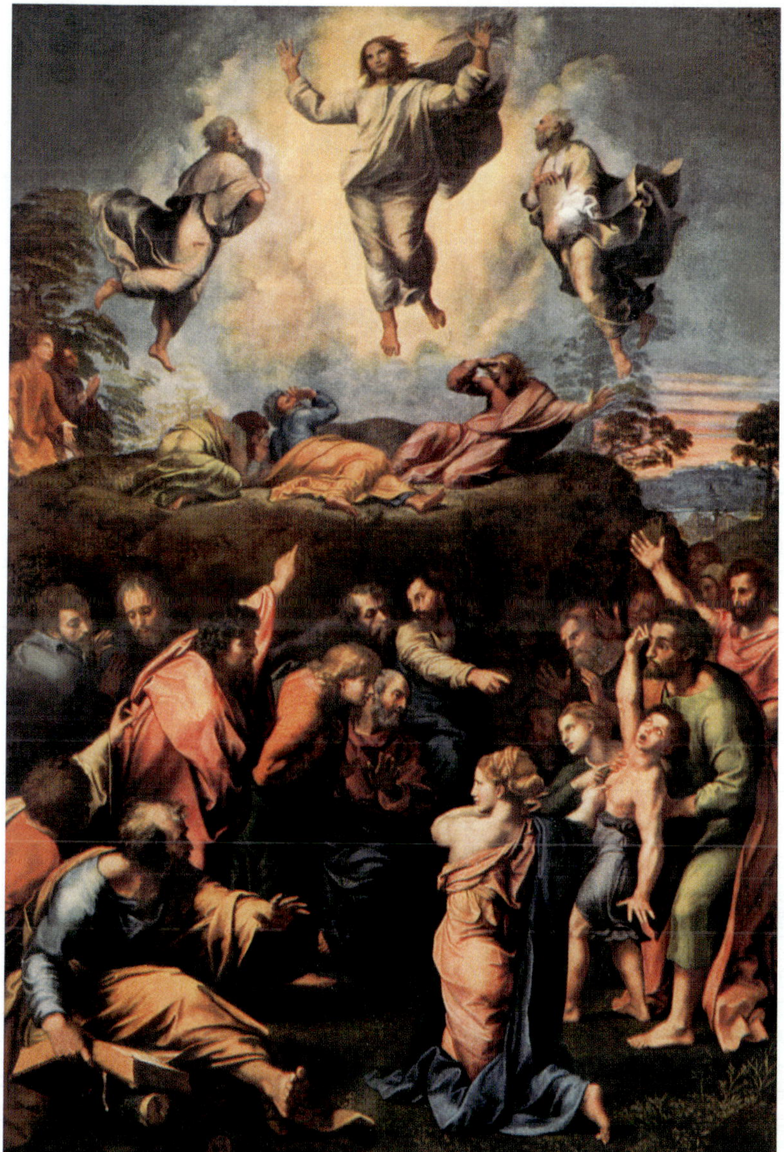

The Transfiguration [La Trasfigurazione] 1519-20
Oil on Panel. Vatican, Rome.